Thanks

Grateful and sincere thanks to my dear friend Jane who typed up all the work without complaint, gave me great support and suggestions combined with lots of humour at all times.

Dedication

This book is dedicated to my treasured family who are always there for me.

The Author

The author taught Art & Design for 33 years in high school and in latter years combined this with working one day per week in a separate unit for post primary pupils with special educational needs.

This continued for two years after retirement. Full retirement led to joining creative writing classes. She was successful in getting work published in many anthologies, as well as reading her work on Ulster Radio, R.T.E. Radio, The Ulster Arts Club, Ormeau Baths Gallery, Crescent Arts Centre, Woodstock Library, Courtyard Theatre at the Mill, Newtownabbey. Some of these readings were due to being a prize-winner e.g. The Charles Macklin Poetry Competition held annually in Culdaff, Co. Donegal.

She received a commission to illustrate a series of books for P1 to P6 primary classes. These dealt with early school issues, respect, loneliness, bullying, fear, happiness and confidence building. This series "Little Pathways" was funded by the Churches Peace Education Programme and was used widely in Northern Ireland primary schools.

Her work involved poetry peace banners spanning the Ormeau Bridge during the Ballynafeigh Peace Project.

Author's work also published in:

'Woodstock Writers'
'Speech Therapy'
'New Poetry from Northern Ireland'
'All on a Misty Morn'
'Abracadabra – Series 1, 2, 3.'
'Alchemy Anthology'
'Home Thoughts Anthology'
'Writers Inc. Anthology'
'New Bridges Anthology'
'Turning Point Anthology'
'George Best Will Not Be Playing Today'
(A book of tributes to George Best)

VICTORIA PLUMS

Warmed by late evening sun, the plums
hang heavy by the pink brick wall.
Lazy bees, weighed down with nectar,
see-saw among the water lilies,
seeking a soft landing,
then drink greedily from the garden pool.
From the window I can smell the roses,
that faint sweet smell of powdered cheeks
of long dead aunts.
the garden seems so still, just nature breathing.
Languidly the wolfhound lifts her head,
long neck craning as she looks about.
Her great grey body heaves from the warm stone,
then, agile as a deer,
she tiptoes up the rockery.
High above the garden she casts a wary eye,
and through the green canopy of leaves
stretches towards the ripened plums.
Unseen, I watch her sucking them in,
golden juices dripping from her jaws,
a guilty silhouette in the fading August night.

THREADS

Holding the photo near, I look into her face
tracing soft sepia features with a finger
wanting to reach her, call her back again
to share the thoughts, the questions never asked,
to re-connect the cord that joined us,
linking our destiny.
But she is beyond this sharing, she is caught
like a knot in her own time warp.
Her pattern is now completed.
The colours of her life selected,
woven into the tapestry of past days.
Now through adult eyes I comprehend
and see her struggles with clarity,
live them, am one with them, mother feeling for mother.
She gazes back, safe inside the starched garb I never knew
armour to face the world, giving her crackling authority.
In this nurse's uniform she is not familiar to me, my mother.
I remember the crossover pinny, in a cloth she called "shower of hail".
I gather my thoughts, longing to communicate once more,
but she stares back at me, beyond recall
while I sit here, untangling my own loom.

Joan Mac Cabe

BIRTHING

Swollen with late autumn heat and rain,
Your rounded shape sings satin brown.
Hectic hues of orange, red and gold
confetti round you as you fall,
a safe landing.
The earth is soft, welcoming, bedding you in.
Within your tight stretched skin
you are longing to split, birthing your seedling.
Spindly and green, still clinging to your husk
it spirals skywards.
As your strength ebbs and dies
the cycle begins.

THE EYE OF THE BEHOLDER

My mother was very much given to trailing round the auction rooms of Belfast, and from a very early age I was bitten by the same bug. Ross's, Morgan's, Smithfield and Grey's were a constant source of wonderment to me, and I always loved the hoking and poking each visit entailed.

One particular day we were in Grey's, which was then situated in Montgomery Street. Now I have only to close my eyes and I am that eight year old child back in the dusty old auction room, with sunlight latticing the mirrors of the ancient ornate sideboards and brass beds, with many a tale to tell, lying abandoned against the back wall. Huge polished wardrobes with misty mirrors reflected my curious face and my mother's familiar shape.

Drawn by all the treasures piled high on every available surface I wandered off, touching an ancient umbrella stand made from an elephants foot here, running my fingers through the dust on a piano there. In a tall glass cabinet I suddenly spied a set of round white plaques. I thought they were made of marble and climbed up on a chair to have a closer look.

There lay at least fourteen of the most beautiful images I have ever seen! In later life I discovered that they were fashioned in Parian ware, but at that moment I was amazed at their perfection and detail. Nymphs and fawns gambolled over the cold white plaques, perfect noses and chins were modelled to last forever in their cool beauty. Delicate tendrils of hair curled and intertwined with flowers and ribbons, and Junoesque goddesses held up fat squirmy cherubs for generations to admire.
I looked and looked and a deep sense of want swamped my soul. I loved every one of them with every fibre of my being but I knew I could never have them. Behind me I was aware of old Mr Grey speaking to my mother, but their conversation hung like a sheet, unheeded above my head. I only had eyes for the beauty before me.

Suddenly he reached past me and opened the door of the glass cabinet. "Do you want to take one out and have a proper look?" he said. It was a dream come true. I chose carefully and held the cold plaque with reverence. It showed a winged goddess, floating through the air and scattering roses as she flew. But best of all she carried a small winged cherub on her cool white shoulder. "Would you think of buying it?" asked Mr Grey, and he and my mother shared a laugh as I had often seen grownups do. I was raging inside, for I knew I had one bare shilling, my pocket money for a week. Silently I pulled it out and offered it to him. Without a word he took the shilling and handed me my treasure. To this day, I still have the plaque, and when I feel its cold white surface and trace the flowing curves of my beautiful goddess, I cannot forget and old man's kindness and understanding.

NIGHT BATHERS

Green water ebbs, flows, absorbs the lovers.
Spangled with phosphorescence, it captures them in its net.
Like white sails, arms break the surface of the water
reaching to one another in benediction.
Stars quilt the sky as they drift on their backs,
silver waves caress them as they clasp hands.
Murmuring secrets, they float together as one.
White bodies curve, pale crescents in the inky water,
to join together, jigsawed by destiny.
They swim in tandem now and time stands still.
Dipped in sea magic their silence is conversation
heard only by these liquid lapping waves.

A CHILD'S WAR

Despite the fact that I was only three, I did realise that the wail of the siren was not to be ignored. When it sounded the grown ups had only one thing to say – "Jerries are coming" followed by a flurry of activity. That struck terror into my heart and a fear that this time they really would capture me and all those dear to me. I wasn't too sure just how this would happen but the choices seemed endless!

My main scenario seemed to picture hundreds of stark black figures holding guns, slowly dropping from above, their white silk parachutes curling and billowing against the inky blue sky. Their faces would be unseen, inscrutable, behind smoky black goggles. Hadn't I seen them myself on the newsreels in the Curzon Cinema, floating down, heads encased in the brown leather flying helmets, ready to murder all before them!

I knew our flat roof over the coal shed was an ideal landing area for them, especially as it overlooked the big house right across the entry. Here a group of Yankees were billeted. Sometimes I stood on the wee iron bed in our return room to watch the Yankees at their work. On a good day they sat outside the kitchen door, peeling what seemed to be a full sack of potatoes and vegetables, laughing and talking in their 'Roy Rogers' voices. Sometimes they drank from funny shaped bottles, tipping back their faces to imbibe the dark liquid, which I later knew to be Coca-Cola.

Now and again they would catch sight of me and would wave in a friendly easy way. I would duck behind the lace curtain, uncertain how to respond, but drawn back to peek again and again, as they worked and whistled cheerfully in the pale afternoon sunshine. As I watched them the thought struck me, would the Jerries know I was friendly with the Yankees? If they did find out I was a goner, for I knew they were sworn enemies. I decided to keep away from the return room window and to mind my own business in future.

Mostly the warning siren sounded at night, and its sound was the signal for our family to leave their beds and to squeeze into the cramped area beneath the stairs. This was reached by a small wooden door wallpapered on the outside to match the kitchen, and rough dark wood on the inside. "Under the stairs" or "the Glory Hole" was the choice of most Belfast families during the air raids of the 1940's. It was considered to be the safest place in the house to shelter from the nightly bombing raids. It was also favoured as a safe storage place for the family treasures. Our house was no exception to this rule, and a motley selection was stored there. I used to love inspecting the old cardboard boxes, with their treasure trove of china, silver and ornaments, all carefully wrapped in pages from the "Ireland's Saturday Night."

Rose flowered cups of fine white china, too precious to be filled with tea and exposed to the hurly-burly of the kitchen, lay quietly redundant in the layers of yellowing newspaper. Nearby was a big cardboard box with the lettering "Sunlight Soap" on its side. It held a great silver teapot, ornate with flowers and leaves, its shiny belly swelling out in pride, holding court with its attendant sugar bowl and milk jug.

One particular night the siren blaring loudly wakened me. In great haste we all tumbled down the stairs and into our "Hidey-hole". As the wee door lay open I watched my father preparing to join the men of our street in their nightly watch. I followed his large shadow moving in the dim candlelight, dreading the moment he would disappear into the unknown, not sure that he would ever come back to us.

At these times my greatest comfort was hugging close our large and extremely fat black cat, Felix, as I sat on the pile of cushions at the back of the stairs. It was the custom during these raids to open the windows and leave the back door ajar, in the hope that the effect of any explosion would be lessened.

Having made these preparations, my mother joined us at last. We lay back among the cushions, eating apples and reading 'Sunny Stories', the 'Dandy' or the "Girls' Crystal", according to our age and stage. Suddenly Felix decided to vacate his cosy seat between my knees and headed for the gap in the door and the freedom of the night. I was too young to know or comprehend the workings of the feline mind, which drove that cat to his nocturnal wanderings. All I felt was the terror in my soul for his safety as he sallied nonchalantly into the hell that was Belfast, that particular night.

I could hear the enemy planes droning overhead, sweeping over the city, I could see the flash of the arc lights searching out the enemy, and hear the odd muffled explosion in the distance. I clapped my hands over my ears as the drone grew louder, and an insane fear for my beloved Felix swamped me. I opened my mouth, screwed up my eyes, and screamed loud and long. No one could pacify me or comfort me, I wanted that cat and nothing else would do!

Finally my mother gave in, and flinging aside the blanket, crawled into the cold and draughty kitchen. Wishing all cats to hell and back, she felt her way into the yard, calling softly to the errant Felix. After what seemed an eternity, the black shape of him danced back up the wall, down onto the mangle and in through the kitchen door. Purposefully, he ran between my legs, tail stiff as a ramrod, and leapt straight into my waiting arms.

Ecstatically I buried my face in his cold musky fur. I could feel the chill and the damp of him against my bare legs. As he settled in my lap a deep resonant purr filtered from his soft body to mine. His claws rhythmically kneaded and worked the arm of my blue woolly jumper as he gave himself up to the warmth of my body. In the soft flicker of the candle I watched his green eyes narrow and close. Together we slept.

WASH DAY

On wash day we were close, partners in preparation,
boiling sheets and pillowcases
"as white as the driven snow"
she said.

In the scullery the stove hissed hot blue flame
as she pummelled with wooden spoon.
"steam rises like prayer"
she said.

Together we stretched the linen,
a winding sheet of childhood dreams.
"cool and fresh as baby's breath"
she said.

Then folding began, me at the end of the yard
struggling to flap the sheet towards the cloudless sky.
"as even as the Seven Mile Straight"
she said.

Then we fed it, dripping, into the maw of the mangle
to emerge in damp folds of cool pressed linen.
"clean enough for the King!"
she said.

On the gray Belfast roofs the small birds sang,
Bangor Blue slates creaking in the heat.
"a grand job, well done"
She said.

Together we pegged the linen on the line.

DECEMBER 1948

As the day darkened she cracked a match,
lighting the hissing mantle above her head.
I stood on a stool at the scullery table,
small hands stretched to stir the sticky dough.
The air was filled with foreign perfume
of cinnamon, ginger, allspice and cloves.
She poured, and a wayward stream of hissing stout
cascaded down those scented valleys.
All knowing, she filled blue-ringed enamel bowls
and crowned them with crisp crackling paper.
"Stand back, stand back," she said,
lowering them into the spitting cauldron
above my head.
Then she sat me on the table, with a handful of currants,
and we listened to the bubbling water,
and the snoring of the collie dog
beneath my feet.

19

EXPECTATIONS

We were 50's girls.
All frilly petticoats and ponytails.
Doe eyes and flirty looks.
Proudly carrying college books,
As we danced along on Louis heels.

Freshly starched and linen pure.
As innocent as May's first butterflies.
Freefalling into adult lives.
Each day just waiting
Especially for us.

And in those carefree days
I shared the dream with you.

BALLYNAFEIGH

On hot June days I trudged to school,
journeying through the Holylands.
Reluctant pilgrim at the end of term,
longing for freedom.
On winter days I rode the tram,
creaking and groaning up to Ballynafeigh.
As the bell tolled twelve I was free to run
down Sunnyside Street, to climb the sticky mountains
of the brickfields.
Happily jumping the hollows filled with rain
I moulded rich red clay with childhood dreams.
Saturday, celebration with sixpence in my hand,
Highland toffee and front stalls in the Curzon,
Then a jungle sortie to the Ormeau Park,
to ride triumphant on those lions of stone.
Still that spirit lives within my soul, carefree,
as I was long ago.

OLD BEARDY

In his chosen doorway he sleeps.
Edging and pushing we hop like
startled birds,
retreating then advancing for a closer look.
The tangled pages of the "Tele"
flutters with each breath
as onion like in layered rags
he slumbers on.
Beneath his head a plastic bag,
stuffed with his life and memories.
A dream pillow no one shares.

Ormeau Road 1946

WAITING

Like a mirror shattered,
my pattern lies in senseless shards
The comfort of familiar skills now gone
I lie, silenced like a monk.
Outside, the boring routine of the ward,
inside, raw colour, noise, this silent scream.
The fiesta of past life whirls on within my mind.
I dance, fling paint on canvas, sing.
Child nurses come, with linen white and cool,
Smiling and nodding, circling round the bed.
Sheets rise and fall like the coming shroud,
then paper like, they fold me into the chair.
Battened down, and belted by the rug
I sit, a model of obedience.
My new friend sits beside me,
Death, holding my hand.

REMEMBERING

Built with softly creaking oak
this old bed was our sea of dreams.
It's cool linen a fresh breeze,
the deep channels of the antique eiderdown
a midnight ocean
moving and gleaming,
as we dipped beneath blue satin.
I remember our heads, cradled on soft down
pillows clouding out this world,
and your young arms,
strong ropes that anchored me
in our sea of dreams.

SEA WOMAN

Cool slab of clay rests in my hands,
teeming with the people of my imagination,
one image crowding the rest, demanding form.
Forward comes the sinuous sea-woman
obscuring the others with her flowing hair,
coiling her way into my heart and hand.
She is trapped in the clay, pleading her release.
out of this solid mass she proudly emerges,
the detail of her slanted eyes, those rounded breasts,
and the wild crown of hair around her head.
Majestically she rises from the tangled seaweed,
body curved above the fan of her swirling tail.
In time I watch her through the spy hole,
serene in the fiery womb of the kiln,
and promise her a sea green lustre glaze,
to crown her beauty for eternity.

GEORGE BEST

Belfast boy, with those azure eyes
and the print of God's thumb on your chin
beneath that dazzling smile,
you captured our hearts.
You were poetry in motion
on those weaving dancing feet,
world icon, our boy, blessed with genius
with Mercury's wings on your heels.
Now a swaying ribbon of grief
weeps along with heaven's tears
as sweet voices ease your passage home.
Even in death, you seduce us
as you are carried high
crowned by fragrant lilies,
and then are laid to rest
in the soft brown earth,
Belfast boy, safe
in your mother's arms.

Laid to Rest - December 3rd 2005

28

THE FIRST MAN

She stood knee deep in the top meadow watching the cows, fat bellies cradled in the tall green grass. They lifted their great heads to look solemnly back, then returned to munching the sweet grass. Watching the silky movement of the meadow in the wind, she noted the fleeting colours of grey, green and silver. An insect tickled her leg and she brushed it away. Her eyes moved to the patchwork of fields and up to the rolling hills beyond. She walked a few paces, drinking it in. The heather had washed the hills with soft purple, easing the aching green of the fields below.

She remembered the time she would have rushed for her paints, to capture its magic. Bitterly she looked at her work worn hands, noting their roughness with a new sadness. They had held no paintbrush for such a long time, except the big distemper brush in the barn, used ritually twice a year to produce an arid white expanse. Again she examined her hands, splaying the long pointed fingers in a fan shape. Mother had been right after all – "He'll squeeze the creativity out of you, girl. You are made of too fine a clay to be tied to yon man."

Clay – she remembered the thrill of her first encounter with it in the pottery room at college, so long ago. That feeling of power, with the cool grey ball of clay in your hands, to make what you would of it, to roll it, cajole it into the shape only you saw in it, and make the dream in your head come true. How sad that life was not so easy to shape. She thought of her final exam piece, the "Mother and Child" – two perfect bodies flowing together, their love caught forever beneath the rich cobalt glaze.

The dry rasp of the farm door broke the silence and she could feel his eye on her. "Quit wool gathering up there, and get in and get the tay on!" he roared. The sunlight caught the ginger bristles on his chin as he scratched and yawned. His great rounded belly swayed and rose under the simmet as he stretched.

"I've a fortune's worth of beasts to see to, while you stand there swaying like Ruth amid the corn! Quit collywobbling and get my grub on the table!" The cattle stood, heads raised and still, large black cut-outs against the pink dawn sky. The great slab of him filled the doorway, and she wondered again why she had married him. His pale blue eyes winked and blinked as he focused on her through the sunlight, and his neck flushed.

'What ails ye, girl?" he bellowed. "Shift yourself down here or the back of my hand will do it for you." "I'm coming," she replied, assuming the shroud of duty. She moved slowly, the cool damp greenness brushing her knees as she made for the house.

The kitchen was dim after the brightness of the sunlight. She put the kettle to boil on the Rayburn stove, and the warm soda farls on the table. He was pulling on his wellingtons, straining forward to work his foot into the boot. The small pink circle on the top of his head was like a monk's tonsure, as he bent to the task. He was showing his age, yet she knew she still looked like a slip of a girl, She wondered if not having children had anything to do with it, maybe it took carrying a child to ripen a woman's body. She pushed the thought away and set the tea and bacon before him. Wedge like, he filled the chair, packing the food into his body as if for a siege. He ate solidly, and then belched noisily. Slapping the cap on his head he half turned at the door. "I'm away to start the milking," he said, and slammed the door.

Silence seeped back into the room and Hannah was glad of it. As she sank into the rocker, she caught sight of the mother and child sculpture on the mantle shelf. On an impulse she lifted it down. Gently she wiped away the film of dust it had gathered, turning its blue perfection this way and that, admiring the full smooth curves of the intertwined bodies.

What dreams she had when this clay was soft and eager to be moulded. This woman was Hannah, and the baby was her child. In those days she saw a baby coming to crown a deep and passionate relationship with a future husband. Then she had no doubt the dream would come true. What age had she been then? Nineteen or twenty? What did it matter now? He had changed, the longed for baby never came, and the dream slowly soured. Her father had been all for the match, influenced by the big farm on the hill, but mother's words had come true. Marriage had brought unwelcome changes into her life. Better to have lived alone than to exist in the shadow of this man. She cursed tradition, that unseen pressure that mocked the unwed, making the single woman an object of pity. At thirty-two she was 'on the shelf' or 'unclaimed treasure' as her Aunt Bessie put it. At a church social he had come into her life, big as a barn door and eager to marry. The Minister had taken her aside to give advice. "He's a fine big man, Hannah, and he'll be a good provider," he said 'Not to mention that grand farm, you couldn't ask for better. I hope you realise how fortunate you are!"

After that the courtship began in earnest, Hannah, flattered by his attention. High tea at the hotel became a regular Friday night event. On Sunday they walked the shore at Castlerock, watching the great waves crashing and foaming onto the sands. It was there he asked her to marry him. Overcome by his urgency, she accepted.

Within a short time the trips ended. The harvest needed saved, a prize cow was calving, or some other business needed his attention. Life narrowed down to the work of the farm. She badly missed her pupils and fellow teachers, and dreaded the long empty evenings when she finished her chores. At night she did her duty, accepting his urgent sex in the blackness of the bedroom. Monthly he questioned her, eagerly at first, then with mounting resentment. He made an appointment with the doctor, sitting in on the consultation. Thorough tests revealed no reason why she should not conceive.
When the doctor gently questioned him, he said he saw no reason to be examined, sure wasn't he the strongest man in the town land? Diplomatically the doctor advised them to let nature take its course.

Hannah tried to turn his resentment away by keeping the house in perfect order, and pandering to his every whim. She baked his favourite soda bread; his shirts and overalls were laundered and folded as soon as he discarded them. She bit her lip when he stamped across the newly washed quarry tiles in his filthy wellingtons. He became an expert at complaining and finding fault, never missing a chance to turn the knife in her wound. He gave her chapter and verse on all the births in the district, noting the sex, weight and lustiness of the infants. Only yesterday he had sat, laden fork halfway to his mouth, and remarked "That wee lassie McAllister married has just produced twin boys for him and her not the size of two turf! I don't know how these wee cutties manage it!" he ventured, with a sly glance at her. There was nothing to say so she left the room and wept. A deep sense of loss and desolation gripped her. If it weren't for the escape in her books she would go mad! Maybe she should cycle into the library. The fresh air would give her a lift. In case he came back to check on her she quickly cleared the table, saving the scraps for the hens. He'd find no fault here if he came back unexpectedly.

The library was quiet today as she browsed along the shelves, selecting her books. On the way out she noticed leaflets on the counter. They listed the night classes starting in the local school. She checked the date of enrolment and made up her mind. She would be at the pottery class!

That evening she told him of her decision. He looked at her in amazement. "Over my dead body!" he roared. "Wasting money and petrol running to a dirty clay class, what benefit would that is to us? Could you not do a home craft class and pick up something useful?" "I am going in on my bicycle." She replied, "And I'm not asking you to pay for the class." He regrouped his thoughts, selecting a familiar theme. "What am I supposed to do while you're out playing with a ball of muck? What about my dinner? I'll be working just as hard on a Wednesday as any other day, and I need my grub!" She looked at him, thinking he could survive for a month on the lard encasing his big frame.

"I'll make sure you don't starve!" she said firmly and left the room. That night he lay in the bed in a huff. Gratefully she accepted the respite, a small battle had been won. On Monday, Hannah enrolled for the class. On Wednesday she played the peacemaker, cooking his favourite irish stew and apple crumble. At the school she found the right room and sat down with the other students. The teacher introduced himself.

"Welcome to the class! My name is Adam Gallagher, the course lasts twelve weeks and I hope you will enjoy it. Don't worry if you haven't done any pottery before, we will all literally muck in together!" A ripple of laughter went round the room. Hannah sat enthralled. She was going to savour every moment of the course. This man was so enthusiastic and helpful she could listen to his soft brogue forever!

Suddenly, he was standing by her table. "Now what sort of pottery are you interested in making?" he asked with a smile. For no known reason Hannah felt vulnerable and exposed.

"I'd love to model a sleeping child, I am really interested in sculpture in clay – what do you think?" she asked. "Certainly, that sounds interesting!" he replied. "It'll be a change from all the pots! I'll sort out some clay for you, maybe one with some grog in it would hold the shape better" Hannah laid her hands on the cold clay and immediately felt the old familiar challenge.

At the end of the class she lovingly wrapped the embryo child in a sheet of plastic and reluctantly placed it in the damp cupboard. If only she could have worked on! Outside, Adam fell into step with her. "Well, were you pleased with your results tonight?" He laughed. "You never lifted your head, and as for tea break!" Hannah flushed, knowing he had read her like a book.

"I just enjoyed every minute! It was like coming home, back to every thing I love!" she said quietly. Adam looked at the transformed face, and was deeply touched. "Great!" he said. "I love to see people enjoying the class, see you next week!"

Hannah cycled home. He was dozing in the rocker as she entered the kitchen. With a grunt he wakened, but did not mention the class. Soon her forgotten skills blossomed with Adam's encouragement. A subtle relationship was growing between them, each week's experiences gathered like perfect beads on a string. Sometimes their hands touched on the clay, and she was swamped by a tide of tenderness and longing. What hung between them was as complex and fragile as a cobweb. Inevitably the last class of the term came, and people drifted out. Hannah's heart lay like a stone in her breast. She wrapped the fat sleeping baby in layers of paper. In the deepening silence of the empty room he came to her and kissed her tenderly. Then he turned her clay-stained hands upwards and cradled them between his own. Unable to speak, they stared into each other's eyes, recognising a deep shared need.

Leaving the school they drove out to the woods south of the town. Hannah cried out with joy as she experienced the tenderness and intensity of his lovemaking. For the first time ever she felt totally fulfilled.

The next Wednesday evening Hannah sat in the rocker, still and quiet in her thoughts. He laid down the paper, unable to contain his curiosity any longer. "Are you not going in tonight?" he ventured. "No" she said. "Not enough people enrolled for the new term, and the teacher's gone home to Sligo." "Do you mean he was a Southerner?" he exclaimed. A torrent of indignant queries lay behind his outburst. Hannah tried to quell the bubble of laughter that threatened to engulf her. "I suppose so." She said mildly. "Good riddance to him!" he snapped. "We want no truck with Free Staters" Hannah hid her smile.

The wintery nights drew in, and she missed her second period. It was no surprise, as she had known instinctively that this child was to be. She cradled her secret joyfully for one more week and then told him. He sat bold upright and then rushed to her. Awkwardly he held her, patting her back with his big ham of a hand.

"Are you really having a babby, after all this time?" he ventured shyly. "Yes, I really am," she said, thinking there was no lie in that statement.

He paced up and down, his feelings naked, leaving him vulnerable and child like before her. "If it's a boy I'll call him William, after me Da!" he said, beaming and rubbing his hands on his backside. She stood up, and it seemed to him that she carried a new air of authority.

"I know in my soul that this baby is a boy," she said "I will call him Adam, after the first man." Marvelling at the change in her he stepped back. Women in her condition were best not crossed. "Well, it's a good old Bible name, after all," he capitulated. "It will suit the lad grand!" He sat down in the rocker, well satisfied with his new status.

11.57PM

Almost midnight and moonlight silvers the earth, gilding the lake and edging scarlet autumn leaves.

Through stiff hoary grasses the black cat slithers, liquid and languid in her pace.

Beneath her velvet paws the startled beetles scuttle to a safer place and the hunter silently moves on.

36

REFLECTION

Ancient bones and seasoned wood creak in friendly unison
as she rocks away the December gloom.
Outside the window a frantic world spins on.
Her company is here, forever smiling
in a careless curve of frames,
a fanfare of past images,
and thoughts of distant days.
In that slow hour between two and three
she tidies an overflowing drawer,
disturbing the layered memories of her life.
Unearthing a lipstick, Coty's "Holly Red"
she paints a Cupid's bow above her crinkled paper chin,
a defiant banner to shock the outside world.
In her head she hears the strains of her favourite waltz
and the swish of the lilac beaded dress she wore.
Raising the mirror she peers at her reflection
remembering her beauty,
on a long forgotten firefly night
in 1927.

BIDDY ANN

Do ye all remember me niece, Biddy Ann?
The proud one that lived above in Glenaan?
The one with the hat with the big cabbage rose?
Wi one skelly eye, and a twist to her nose?
Ye remember her now, sure ye couldn't forget
wi' her wee wobbly chin, like a jelly half set.
The countryside knew that she wanted a man
with a good puck of money, and plenty of land.
So she hunted the dance halls for ten years or more,
and waltzed till the balls of her feet grew so sore
she was forced to go home in big Jamesies' taxi
and soak yon sore feet in the outside yard jaxi.
There she sat on the board and swore at the moon,
she'd jump under a train if she didn't wed soon.
So she plotted and schemed, and hatched a fine plan,
for she was determined to capture a man!
She made a long list of the men not yet claimed,
including the deaf, the blind and the lamed.
Then she looked them all up and looked them all down,
on a Saturday night at the pub in the town.
But one was too fat and one was too thin,
and one looked a fright without his teeth in.
Then a stranger strode in, he came from afar,
and he asked for a pint, up at the bar.
He said he had bought Mickey Doherty's farm
and planned before winter to be settled and warm.
With the stock up and running, and all in its place,
he said to the crowd, with a smile on his face.
Biddy sat tight in the snug by the corner,
she thought straight away he was the man for her.

So she sidled right up to the bar with a smile,
saying she thought she would stay for a while.
She smirked and smiled as she twiddled her hair
and pressed up to him, as he sat in the chair.
She asked for a lift home in his pony and cart,
in the hope he'd be pricked by Cupid's sharp dart.
For six months or more she kept up the pressure
to make bloody sure he'd be banjaxed without her.
A bombardment of farls, buns and tarts wore him down,
till Biddy was sure of wearing that gown.
So finally on the first day in June
they wed, and left for a sweet honeymoon.
Now when they got back it was grand, for a while,
as Biddy played wife with an innocent smile.
A clean shining house with the fire burning bright
and straight up the stairs at the end of the night.
At seven a.m. it was work on the farm,
while Biddy snoozed on, so cosy and warm.
An so it went on both without and within,
the poor man a shadow, so white and so thin.
Worn to the bone with work and bad weather,
the Craytur soon came to the end of his tether.
As he laid himself down he turned, and he said
"You've worked me to death in the fields and the bed.
With God or the Divil I'd much rather sup,"
then he turned to the wall and the ghost he gave up.
To his grave he was taken, in pony and cart,
with Biddy in tears and a hand on her heart.
A tear in her eye and a drip at her nose,
the envy of many, in sad widow pose.
For Biddy came into the money and farm,
with a strapping farm hand, to keep her from harm.
And they say on cold nights there's a creak at her door,
and the patter of warm feet on her bedroom floor.

BY STRANGFORD LOUGH

By the rich crust of seaweed, black-green and dense,
roots tangling in the foam, I search.
Hunting sea treasure, the glittering glass
I gather to light dim winter days.
Crystal, aqua, earth brown and rare blue,
I covet all, sifting pieces smoothed by
the cold green waters of the Lough.
The foaming sea breaks on the rocks of my heels,
then lovingly swirls to suck my toes like a pet dog.
Back aching, I rest, watching a swooping gull
till the clear sweet music of the wind
 sifts my hair, as gently as a lover,
by Strangford Lough.

ORMEAU PARK, OCTOBER 2006

Underfoot ten thousand leaves,
safe haven for the woodland creatures.
I hear their secret comings and goings
in the silence of this early morning.
In the hollowed path soft mist enfolds me,
caresses me, conceals me,
intruder in this hidden world.

ORMEAU PARK

Subversive Nature relentlessly pushes beneath the frozen soil.
Weaving her magic, she pulses life into the dormant world below.
Then between cracked frosted clods of earth
a green shoot creeps, the first thin flag of Spring.
The Crocus follows, a curve of purple crowding the path.
Then come the scented daffodils beneath the oaks,
a swirling river of white and yellow heads.
mirroring the Lagan flowing down below.
Last week sullen black branches scratched a leaden sky.
Now tight wrapped buds relax, and the first leaves,
wrinkled like premature flesh, soften and open to form
a canopy of heartache green above my head.
By the gate two cherry trees stand sentinel,
a sea of pink frothing above their outstretched branches.
light headed blossoms, giddy in the warmth of sudden sun,
in Ormeau Park.

FRIDAY AFTERNOON

Chrysanthemum heads bend over drawing boards
echoing autumn colours of flame and gold and brown.
We are at one in this sun-moted room, comfortable
As we freewheel together down this Friday afternoon.
I pad between their tables, stroking green plants,
breathing deep the scent of lemon verbena,
and listening to the plop of paintbrushes
as colours swirl and blend in the rainbow jars.
Past efforts line the walls, telling their lives and loves,
These half-women, teetering on the brink of life.
The last bell clangs, fracturing our peace.
Chairs scrape and groan and paintings sigh
as they are laid to dry on the dusty benches.
Bags swing as smiling girls wave and rush away.
Fast footsteps echo down the back stairs,
And the silent Art Room seems so empty
On this Friday afternoon.

APPROACHING GLENSHANE

Above the farmhouse, wedged in the hip of the hill
green pines shelter drifting sheep.

Soft rounded rain clouds rest breast like on the mountain,
easing the starkness of this winter.

Sheep bundle together, with backs "Bizarre", patterned
with exclamation marks of red and yellow,

a restless living work of modern art
displayed against the monochrome hill.

In the sodden green below the barn
the hungry cattle cluster round the hay,

Great heads bent in unison to the task,
A secret society, indifferent to my world.

Edging the field, the boiling river foams
Cream and brown, greedy, suckling the bank,

Leaving Glenshane

MIDWINTER IN GLENSHANE

On the high moon plains of Glenshane
sheep hunker against the winter lace of hedges,
while bruised yellow clouds sag over claggy earth,
pock-marked by pools of brown bog water.
On the ridge a scarecrow, dressed in cast-offs,
looms spectre-like on the barren hill.
Against the sky skeleton trees stand,
while the weak December sun stripes the field
with white frost and black shadow,
an unexpected pastoral keyboard.
Deep in the valley the river twists and turns,
Sucking the liquorice rocks in its paths,
And a velvet crow wheels above Glenshane.

RETURN TO GLENSHANE

Pale grey hills merge with darkening sky,
splintered by sighing pines, crowding close.
Plants on a deserted roof bend and twist,
carved by a keening wind.
Below, the wandering ribbon river winds,
ruptured by ancient granite stones.
In soft hollows, cows lie among the rushes
springing from velvet moss.
Sheep crowd the wire fence,
white bumps on textured sand.
Above, birds rise and fall,
black markers in the sky.
Electric pylons, upraised in supplication
like crosses, sanctify this barren landscape.
Then the quarry with its crane, gaunt
Like an old man waiting for the end.
Above me near the road, a lamb,
unsteady on black crayon legs,
calls for his mother
in Glenshane.

50

"THERE'S NO PLACE LIKE HOME"

Ellen plumped down on the old blue chair. Hard as it was, she preferred it to the soft old sofa in the parlour room beyond. She smiled to herself as she thought "What a daft colour to paint a kitchen chair!" Painting it blue was part of the young one's effort to modernise the kitchen all those years ago.

She gave an involuntary glance at the photos on the shelf above the range. As she looked at the familiar faces, a tear slowly slid down her cheek and bounced unheeded onto the back of her hand, to trickle out its life on the navy print apron that encased Ellen's ample body.

Where were they all now? Would there really be a glorious re-union after death with the dear ones – or was it all a big con, with nothing but the fuzzy blackness of the grave at the end of it all? Ellen caught sight of her roughened hands nestled in her lap. The skin around the thumb caught and snagged as she reached into her pocket for a hanky. She examined the hands at close quarters; a good rub of Vaseline would do them a power of good! She laughed as she thought of the magazine article she had read, advertising some expensive hand cream, applied at night and covered by a pair of white cotton gloves! What would they be at next? White cotton gloves! Why the last time she saw a pair of them was about 1949. Doris Day and Debbie Reynolds used to wear them in all those old films. Come to think of it, one of those old films was playing on the TV the last day she visited Maude in the home. Disturbing images of that afternoon floated in soft focus behind her tired lids. All the old grey heads nodding, bobbing or falling as Doris relentlessly sang on about how much she loved the "Black Hills of Dakota!"

She could see them all now, arranged around the day room, neat rows of pale elderly dolls, bibbed and tuckered, ready for afternoon tea, while the child nurses flitted about, regulation plates of biscuits in hand.

Ellen shivered and pushed the images away. She looked at the range, drawn by the aroma of the delicious sultana tea bread. Easing herself out of the chair she crossed to the range. She lifted the tea bread out and tipped it onto the wire tray to cool.

Sweet scented curls of steam rose to cloud her glasses, as she set the wire tray on the draining board. Humming to herself, she lifted out the flower-sprigged cups and set them on the white tablecloth. Next she put out the pot of bramble jelly, a last reminder of a happy sunny September day. The tea bread and a fat slab of yellow butter completed the appetising scene.

Just then the wag-at-the-wall struck four, the tick of the old clock seemed unusually loud today, and it echoed the beating of her heart. Ellen watched the minutes tick by, and a faint sense of unease seeped through her mind.

Just then the doorbell ripped through her thoughts. Decisively, Ellen moved to open the door to her visitor. "Come in, come in, m'dear, what a chilly miserable day," Ellen said as she bustled her visitor into the warm kitchen. "I'll just wet a wee pot of tea to warm you up, and you must have a slice of my special tea bread, – sure it's only out of the oven!"

The visitor looked longingly at the warm currant slices, and thoughts of the diet she had started again on Monday vanished. "Oh, go on, Ellen" she said, "I'd love to sample your delicious baking." She sank down on the old chair and watched Ellen bustling about the kitchen. She was exhausted, this day had required a lot of planning, and she would be glad when it was over. She was surprised by Ellen's cheery manner, such a contrast to her last visit.

Each bite of the buttery tea bread combined delightfully with the hot fragrant tea, as she scoffed the two generous slices on the sprigged tea plate. "Ellen are you not having some yourself?" she said, "It's really delicious!" Ellen smiled and shook her head. She had to admit it, the tea bread was really delicious and the scent of it was so tempting, it was all she could do to resist it. "Would you take another wee slice?" she asked her visitor. After a moment's hesitation, her reply came, "Oh well, I may as well be hung for a sheep as a lamb – but just a small slice mind!" Ellen cut another generous slice, buttered it and watched the visitor wolfing it down. "I see you have your case packed and ready in the hall" she said, between bites. "I'm so glad you have seen sense at last, and I feel ……."

Ellen never did find out what the visitor felt, for at that precise moment a surprised look came over her face, as she slid slowly from the chair, the last piece of tea bread halfway to her open mouth. She settled quietly on the flagged floor and lay quite still.

Ellen peered down at her for a moment, and then she hurried to the cupboard under the stairs and fetched the dustpan and broom. She swept up every crumb and then set the rest of the tea bread on the dustpan. With a practised flick she lifted the iron plate off the top of the range, and dropped the contents of the dustpan into the red-hot heart of the coals. "What a waste of good food," she remarked, as she watched it flare and burn.

She washed the teacups and put away the bramble jelly and the butter dish in the pantry. The kitchen was clean and tidy once again except for the large still body by the table. Ellen paused and looked back as she opened the kitchen door – "I'll sort you out in a moment m'dear," she said kindly. Ellen had her story ready – and it was fool proof! The verdict would be accidental death for no trace of her remedy would ever be found, and who would suspect a vague old lady like herself, especially as she was deemed unable to survive on her own?

Ellen closed the kitchen door firmly and picked up the empty suitcase that sat in the hall. She really wouldn't be needing it ever again, or the place that the Social Worker had reserved for her in that "Home." There was no way she would ever leave her happy little nest with all its memories. They could do what they liked – she would still outfox them all! With a step as light as her heart, Ellen came down the familiar stairs to report the tragedy to the appropriate authorities.

THE BAG

He keeps them in a leather bag,
love-letters full of pressed flowers and promises,
the passionate whispers of their past,
lying beneath a curl of her hair,
among the rainbow stamps.

The drift of perfume she once used
rises to lure him once again,
as his fingers sift and stroke
the web of words she once wrote
to tangle his heart.

In the fading light he empties the bag,
her letters spiral and fall like petals.
The match cracks loudly in the empty room.
Flames leap, twisting her promises,
as words flare and fade in the flames.

The black ash curls and falls.
He is alone and empty as the bag.

THE SIR JOHN LAVERY EXHIBITION. NOV. 2003

I wander through the peaceful gallery
absorbing the details of his life,
longing to walk his sunlit orchard
and this exotic Tangier Street.
Then a cold wind blows from his Swiss mountain,
a miracle of light and shade,
blue shadow and white sunlight
that dazzles and delights my eager eye.
Voyeur-like I pore over his beloved Hazel,
breath taking in her green organza gown,
with titian highlights in her fiery hair,
and daughter Eileen, whose loving hands,
forever clasp her new born girl
amid soft drifts of linen
flowing from her father's brush.

THE LETTER

Once again Billy re-read the letter. There it was in front of him in plain black and white….. You have been admitted to the Teacher Training Course for the academic year beginning September 1st 1936. Please present yourself promptly at….. the rest of the words faded as he hugged his hard won success to himself. Carefully he worked up lather in the wee blue bowl and started to shave around the smile on his face. He thought of the nights he has spent studying at the Technical College, then walking home in the sleeting rain to save the tram fare for books. Well, it had paid off now and no mistake! "Billy, shift yourself on down here," his mother called, "It's gone seven o'clock." Downstairs his mother looked at him sideways as she set the porridge on the table.

"Will ye tell him today, before that letter burns a hole in your pocket, don't leave it any longer son." "Don't you know rightly I'll have to let him know today," Billy snapped. He touched his mother's arm, "I'm sorry for biting your head off – it's just that I'm on edge over it all. I can't believe the letter has actually come, and I don't relish the thought of telling Mr Stewart." Billy bent to lace up his boots. "He dropped a few hints about promoting me up to the office, so this news will spoil his plans and he doesn't like to be crossed!" His mother handed him his lunch tin. Then, on a rare impulse she caught him round the shoulders and kissed his cheek. "Good luck son," she said.

Billy pulled the door after him, warmed by her unexpected gesture. He stood looking down the street. Above the chimneys he could see the great red hulk of the mill, Lord and Master of all. Maybe he would write a poem about it. Cheerfully he marched down the middle of the road, his boots ringing on the cobbles. Other workers trickled into step from the little side streets. In the light of the gas lamps their faces were caught white and flat, fish on a slab. For them it was just another day at the factory, another backbreaking day of toil. Billy's heart gave a lurch of joy as he felt the letter inside his jacket. He'd be leaving this dreary morning pilgrimage behind and spending all his time at the books, soon, soon.

He quickened his step as he spied Rose turning the corner ahead. She was wearing a navy dress with white dots all over it, a pattern his mother called 'shower of hail'. "Rose, Rose" he murmured to himself. He was secretly mad about her hair, about all of her. Well maybe now he might get up the courage to ask her to the pictures or maybe a Sunday walk up the Cave Hill. The thought excited him and gave him strength for the task to come. As Billy filed through the gate with the other workers, his resolve strengthened. "I'll go up and tell him at the morning break" he told himself.

The usual morning rush ebbed and flowed. He kept busy running with supplies for the looms, and hauling the baskets back to stores. The clatter of the machines and the chatter of the workers filled the air. Over the great webs of linen he caught sight of Rose and she smiled at him.

At ten thirty sharp the factory horn sounded and Billy headed for the office. A few curious heads turned but the workers were making the most of their break, drinking tea and eating part of their piece from their lunch tins. He tapped the door of the office and waited.

"Come in," barked Mr Stewart "and close that bloody door tight, there's a draught that would cut the legs from under you today." It was obvious he was in a foul mood. He stood near the window keeping one eye on the workers below, and the other on the office clock. He was a stickler for time and not a moment more would they get, if he had his way. He swung back to Billy. "Well lad, what do you want? Spit it out, time is money you know." Billy quietly handed him the letter and waited for all hell to let loose. It was not long in coming. He could see Stewart was working himself up into a froth, his face purpling and his lips moving as he scanned the letter. He pulled his glasses off and waved the paper in the air. "Well that beats Bannagher!" He roared. "You? Teacher Training College, no less, and me thinking of doing you a favour by upping you to the office!" Billy stood his ground. Stewart peered again at the letter. "I suppose the mill office would be the halfpenny place now to put you?" he roared. "Let me tell you pipsqueak, it's too bloody good for the likes of you." He looked over at Miss Rice to gauge her reaction. She sat at the high desk, head bent over the ledger, betrayed only by the two high spots of colour on her cheeks. It seemed as if she was oblivious to these extraordinary events, as her pen squeaked industriously across the yellow pages.

Stewart fixed his eye on Billy once again. "Are you determined to go on to this college then, throwing away the good job you have here, and a chance at a better one if you behave yourself?' "I am," said Billy "and I would like to thank you for the offer though I…" Stewart didn't give Billy a chance. "Away on back to your work while you have it" he roared, hustling Billy out to the office stairs," and good luck to them idiots if they think they can make a Master out of you, God help their wit." His angry voice bounced from loom to loom as his words began to register on the faces of the workers.

The women began to titter among themselves, their voices rising above the clatter of the looms. "Sweet William, is it a teacher you're going to be?" called Sarah Bennett, as Billy came down the office steps. "Not good enough Sarah" jibed Maggie Rice, "Our Bill's going to be a professor – a loony professor!" Their squeals and crackles echoed up to the rafters of the mill. On the pretext of joining a thread Sarah ducked round to her cronies, her broad feet splashing in the puddles on the floor.

"I'd love to give Professor Billy a wee lesson myself – what about lunchtime?" She whispered to the three eager faces. Nodding and tittering they turned back to the clacking looms.

At 1pm the hooter broke through the din of the factory floor. Sarah winked at the others and led the procession out to the yard. Most of the workers were taking advantage of the early June sunshine, legs stretched out, backs supported by the factory wall as they ate their piece. Billy had positioned himself on a pile of sacking near the yarn store. From this spot he could see Rose eating her food with another girl, and he reckoned that she would have to pass him sooner or later. Now and again he caught her glance, and knew with triumph that she was aware of him. A bubble of excitement swelled inside him – maybe he would ask her out to the pictures on Saturday night? He was certainly on a different footing now that he was going into teacher training, and he knew her Da would now welcome him.

A dark shadow blotted out the sunlight and his thoughts. He looked up at the circle of females above him. Maisie leaned down and poked him. "Billy, our wee Mr Brainbox, are you leaving us to go and teach the wains?" she shrieked. "How many beans make five, sweet William? Called big Maureen, folding her arms across her flowery chest. Billy felt helpless. On and on they catcalled, closing in the circle as they chanted. "I'd like to see the teacher" minced one of the girls. "Well dear, you shall see him immediately!" squealed another. "Off with his trousers!"

As one, they rushed at Billy, who fell backwards, his foot caught in a pile of sacking. An unreasonable and unquenchable fear gripped him, as he felt the hands plucking and pulling at him. Sweat broke on him and a hot tide of shame swept his body as he felt his garments yanked from around his ankles. Helpless as a baby, they held him down, and with a cry of triumph swung his trousers high in the air. He scrabbled frantically to cover himself with the sacking, but he was dragged up and hoisted high as thy paraded him round and round the yard. He was conscious of so many sensations, the cool air on his nakedness, the pale sky above him, the white face of Rose caught at a curious angle. Anger, rage and deep boiling hatred seethed within him.

From the office window Mr Stewart looked out to see what the commotion was all about. As if in slow motion he watched Billy being bounced about above the shoulders of the women. He saw Sarah's foot catch in the sacking and he saw Billy fall from their shoulders into the space between them. He ran for the stairs shouting, "Ye wee bitches, you've done for him! Get out of my road and get help!" They scrambled to their feet protesting that he was alright, but as they regrouped, silence fell.

Billy lay where he had fallen, his face ashen, his naked body curled awkwardly on the grey flags of the yard. "Jesus, we never meant to hurt the wee lad, it was all meant to be a bit of fun," whimpered Sarah. "Somebody get a blanket."

Billy didn't hear the ambulance coming. But in the hospital he did hear the 'Big Doctor" tell his circle of students, who were standing respectfully round the bed, "His mobility may be compromised. We need his x-rays as soon as possible. The injury depends on the way the patient falls."

These days his Ma parks the chair near the parlour window so that he can see what's going on. If there's a wee blink of sun she pushes him out to the front door, well tucked up, then he can look up and down the street. The children stop and talk to him on their way home from school, he likes that, it makes his day. Sometimes he wishes he still had the letter, to take a wee juke at it, but it rotted away where it lay on the cobbles.

STUDENT LOVERS

Winter sun, hanging low, red glowing,
while frost ices the station bench.
The Guildhall clock now splintering
the silence of the morning.
I am alone in the waiting room
when they come, eyes red, arms entwined,
caught in a web of misery.
They seek the darkest corner,
retreating from the coming parting.
I hear confessional whispering,
and the soft suck of flesh on flesh.
As she weeps, he licks her tears,
hands seeking hands, a desperate communion.
The bus groans in, and I leave this room,
wondering which lover will follow.
From the window I see their last kiss,
as he caresses curling titian hair.
Then, forehead pressed to forehead,
they share silent thoughts.
The driver shifts, then coughs,
and now she stands alone.
Hands pressed together through cold glass,
reflect twin images of despair.
As the bus swings out along the Foyle
we both look back, and see her standing there.

FIRST LOVE

In hot August sun we worked the whispering field,
cutting, gathering and stooking ripe corn.
I remember the crack of dry stalks underfoot,
and the full sheaves of grain in my arms.
Dust eddied, shimmering in bright sunlight
and field creatures bolted for long grass.
In late afternoon the women brought tea
and the jade-eyed girl came last of all,
swaying with the heavy basket on her hip.
We sat apart among the yellow stooks
drinking strong tea, drinking one another in.
As she turned I saw the silken chaff
caught between her milk white breasts,
and I sat silenced by her beauty.
Then the fiddler rosined his thready bow
and dream notes spiralled out,
catching us fish-like in their magic mesh.
When the dancing began she came slowly to me,
Through the cotton I felt the warmth of her flesh,
and when she turned those eyes on me
I knew that she was mine.

THE ENCOUNTER

That spring a young man came to town
the sky was azure, like her gown.
He walked the road as she rode by
and as she passed he heard her sigh.
"What wouldn't I give for a man of my own?
For him I would give up yon castle, my home.
I would spoil him, caress him, give him my love,
lie with him yonder, beneath stars above.
I'd feed him with ripe fruits, filling his mouth.
I would ride with him into warm winds in the south.
With him on the soft silver sand I would lie,
holding him close as the sea birds flew by.
I would cradle his head on my soft naked breast
in a boat, as I rocked him so gently to rest.
As I gaze down at him with a finger I'd trace
the planes and curves of my dear lover's face,
then I'd wrap him in swansdown and carry him home
wearing my blue gown, on the back of the roan."
The young man looked up with a smile on his face
and he thought that this town was a bloody odd place.
His Ma often warned him about girls such as this,
who were out to corrupt him, just like this young Miss.
"Me dear, if you don't mind I'll just pass on by,
for on yonder wet sand I've no wish to lie,
and as for the boat," he said with a frown, "When it
goes up, my stomach goes down.
I'm happy to live with me Ma on the farm
and I know in the country I'll come to no harm.
So just gather up your bonny blue gown,
and I'll herd me pigs to the market in town."

SEDUCTION

Remember the heavy scents of autumn,
wet clay and drying flowers,
closing your eyes over bucky roses
seducing with their last perfume,
spinning dreams in your head,
then running barefoot on sherbet green grass,
still clinging to a fading summer.

SPIDER'S WEB

Irish lace bed spreading the misty November hedge
hangs, suspended in its own green canopy.
My breath forms another quilt,
ethereal, mist floating
in cool winter sunshine
as I peer in wonder at perfection.
Then nature gilds the lily
with a single dew-drop,
glimmering and shimmering in your fragile web,
while you, on long dancer's legs
quickstep up the frosted hedge,
leaving me in awe of your creation
in the stillness of this morning.

HEALING

I was the wordless watcher by the door.
Choked with emotion, filled with awe
as thin brown hands curved
to cradle the red gold head.
Whispering his ancient lore
into the small pink ear,
rocking the child with reverence
as he hunkered on the floor.
Layer on layer peace settled
and piercing screams ended.
Tender loving hands
trace his tiny frame,
secret whispers still shared
as garments are restored.
Reverently he places the baby
in the crook of his mother's arm.
a tired Indian youth then smiles,
and leaves us, humbled, in this quiet hospital room.

MOSAIC MAKER

By the rich crust of seaweed, black-green and dense,
roots tangling in the foam, I search
hunting sea treasure, the glittering glass
I gather to light dim winter days.
Crystal, aqua, earth brown and rare blue,
I covet all, sifting the pieces smoothed by
the cold green waters of the Lough.
The foaming sea breaks on the rocks of my heels,
then lovingly swirls to suck my toes like a pet dog.
Back aching, I rest, watching a swooping gull
till the clear sweet music of the wind
lifts my hair, as gently as a lover,
by Strangford Lough.

LOST OPPORTUNITY

William worked quietly with the ease that comes from the constant repetition of familiar tasks. Soft autumn shafts of sunlight caught and enriched the russet backs of his cows as they patiently waited their turn to be milked. Normally, he revelled in the peace of this time of the day, but this evening his mind was on other matters.

What was he going to say to Biddie? How should he put his case? How could he go up to the big match in Belfast without her tagging along? He dreaded the moment when he would tell her, but equally dreaded the dreary round of the shops that would follow if she came up with him. In a moment of decision he made up his mind. He was determined to have the day away, come hell or high water and this evening he would tell her.

The bulk of the work now done, he rested against the rough wall of the shed, and considered the enigma that was Biddie. It still amazed him that after all these years he still didn't know how her mind worked. He wondered if most women were as deep as she was. Certainly in the early years there had been a bit of fun, shared laughter and confidences in the dark warmth of the big old bed. But those days were long gone, and she kept herself to herself and spoke little. He thought again of those early years, full of promise, waiting eagerly for news of a child, a son, who would work side by side with him on the land, as he had done with his own father. But month followed month, and year followed year and no child came. Biddie turned her face to the wall, unable or unwilling to share the grief that lay between them. She shut out the questions in his eyes, and busied herself, the house her shrine.

Everything had to be perfect, it was as if she sought solace from the row of pristine pans, the cupboard full of jams and jellies, the tidy linen cupboard with its contents folded to perfection, and the spotless tiles of the kitchen floor, washed daily as if in some penitential rite.

God – how he longed for a bit of diversion in his life. The day away at the match would straighten him out; give him something to enjoy, to think back on. Maybe Biddie would even come out of her shell and ask a few questions about the day. He might get a wee box of the special toffees from that shop in the town that she always insisted on going to – that would maybe please her.

Anyway, it would be grand to sit on the train, free of responsibility for the day, looking around the faces on the carriage, weaving stories around them, wondering about their lives and loves. Biddie could manage rightly for the day – let her forget the damned house and see to the animals.

He thought of the bright green fields, the soft grey mountains, the animals in the pasture and the other men's' farms, the soft tapestry that lay between Ballymena and Belfast. His heartbeat quickened and he headed towards the kitchen door, with his mind made up.

Biddie was busy, setting the food on the table managing not to catch his eye as she walked back and forth to the scullery. Then she settled herself in the chair by the warm range. "Have you heard if any of the neighbours are going up to the big match in Belfast this Saturday?" she suddenly asked.

William could hardly believe his luck, here was Biddie starting the very conversation he had gone over in his head not five minutes since. "I'm thinking of going up myself with some of the men. You'll be grand here for the day, just feed the animals and don't take any heed of the house for one day."

The room was very quiet except for the tick of the old clock on the back wall. William slid a glance over at Biddie to see what the reaction was, but she kept her head bent over the knitting, though her fingers were still. He started to gather up the dishes and she immediately moved to wash, dry and tidy away the delph. When all was done she left the room, and he knew she was in the bedroom.

Irritated, he thought about her reaction, and the lack of communication between them. When the footsteps ceased in the room above, he went up the stairs and got the brown tweed suit out of the wardrobe in the spare room. Carefully he draped it over the rail of the stairs to let the warmth from the kitchen below air it, and soften the reek of the mothballs which rose to his nose.

Through the jamb of the door he peeked into the bedroom to see which way the land lay. There wasn't a move out of Biddie, she lay as neat as a corpse beneath the hand-stitched coverlet, with her head facing the wall. After a decent interval, William slid into bed, taking care to leave a space between them. He toyed with the idea of casually dropping his arm across her waist, hoping she would turn and share a bit of talk with him. But Biddie kept her distance and in a fit of silent temper he decided to let her sulk in solitude. Tomorrow would be a breathing space, a day free from her silence and moods.

Biddie was setting down a plate of bacon, eggs and wheaten bread as William came into the kitchen. A thick heavy curtain of silence lay between them. He began to talk in short bursts, forcing an air of normality, forecasting the result of the match, who would score the goals, and what time he expected to be home. "Well, the auld clock says time to go, mind you don't overdo it today" he said. Unexpectedly, Biddie laughed, and he remembered other times and other days of laughter. But he didn't dwell on it, he had to get to the station.

It was grand at Ballymena station – steam already rising from the train. All the men from the surrounding villages piling into the carriages together, and a sense of camaraderie soon enveloped William and his companions. William rarely drank, but when the lads suggested a pint he accepted and joined in the chat. He hadn't realised what a grand bunch of fellows they were! God – wasn't it great, all men together, and plenty of craic to while away the miles.

When they arrived at Great Victoria Street station they decided to go into the town to eat and have another drink, before going to the match. William was very impressed by the Crown Bar and joined in the conversation as they all piled in, jostling, laughing and calling for a pint all round. Pipes were lit, and laughter rang out as the dark creamy liquid emptied from the big glasses.

William was entranced! Here he was in a fancy bar in Belfast, surrounded by good pals, with the rest of the day and the match to look forward to. What opulence surrounded him, the gleaming tiles, the soft red velvet seats, the polished wood and the fine brass lamps and mirrors of the Crown were a far cry from the wee bar he visited the odd time he was in Ballymena. When he came back from the lavatory two men spoke over to him – "Up for a day in the big smoke?" William answered eagerly and in no time at all they were swopping yarns and pints. By now he was feeling light-headed and began to look around the bar for his own mates. Not a one was to be seen, as William scanned the snugs and the far corners of the big bar. They must have set out for the match while he was sitting, half stupid, in the toilet. What was he to do now? Truth to tell, he only had a vague notion of how to get to the match, and he was too proud to ask anybody about here.

By now the two local men had moved on, and William sat alone in the snug, wondering what to do. He felt such a fool, but was reluctant to leave, telling himself you needed to be careful in these times. He wondered what Biddie might be doing and with a shock discovered it was 3.30pm by the big clock behind the bar. It was too late now to try to get to the match so he ordered another drink and then another.

A feeling of melancholia overcame him, and as if through a telescope he looked back down the days of his marriage, the shared loneliness, the drifting apart. He wondered how two people could live and sleep, eat and breathe the same air and yet be so far apart. How had it happened to them? William felt tears welling in his eyes so he rested his head on his arm, carefully turning it away from the entrance to the snug.

He needn't have worried, it was that slack time before the evening rush began, and the bar was almost empty. The barmen bustled about, collecting glasses, wiping tables and generally preparing for the evening rush. William slowly drifted into a dim world of distant sounds, the clinking of glasses and bottles, and the background music of a radio at the back of the bar. Senses dulled by the unfamiliar alcohol, he slept soundly, oblivious of the pool of spilt stout slowly soaking into his sleeve.

William remembered little of his friends half carrying, half hauling him back to the station to catch the train home. He remembered even less of the journey back to Ballymena, just the sweet sensation of lying across the seat in the train and drifting back into unconsciousness.

Eventually they arrived and the shock of the sharp night air roused William sufficiently to realise that he was home. As his companions held him up, his eyes brought Biddy's shocked face into focus. "Drink." she thought. "He's in the horrors of drink." She watched as thy let him down into the chair, still staring at him as if he was some kind of monster, an alien in her world. William's eyes found hers again. In the silence of the moment he rose and lurched unsteadily towards her, a mute supplication, a plea for understanding in his eyes. Stricken, she spun around and rushed from the room.

DANISH MEADOW

Head dizzy with sweet summer scents I walk this field,
the hot sun now a hand print on my back.
Interlaced with flowers, green weeds yield
to brazen poppies, blazing out a track.
Insects hover, swaying above tall grass,
their secret language buzzing in my head.
Like petals floating round me as I pass
soft clouds of butterflies are rising from their bed.
Great dragonflies from secret places fly
on stained glass wings to skim the poppies red,
while down beneath lush grass black ants crawl by,
their secret world invaded by my tread.

42 NORTH PARADE

The house still stands, living and breathing
stair still creaking
remembering the small boy stretching and growing
words spinning round in his head.
In quiet corners
Layered memories are living,
my heart hears them sighing and singing
telling the story of a poet in the making.
From your window I see the white lilac
still blooming,
the same small birds are still singing.
The house is now waiting,
its heart is still beating
for the soul it once nurtured,
someday to return.

A poem written for the Belfast poet Tom Paulin
who grew up in this house, my home since 1969.

AUTUMN

Sucking her breath in she blows a coolness
beneath her canopy of swirling leaves,
slowly building a crunching carpet beneath her skirts,
then whirls and twirls,
scudding through the creaking branches.
With a soft sigh she questions her fading beauty,
then, in denial, scatters ripe satin chestnuts
among the scarlet leaves below.
Carelessly lifting them, she re-arranges them
in hectic pattern, worthy of Matisse.

BABY OF BETHLEHEM

He came in the stillness of the evening
as a star lit the desert sky,
piercing the velvet of the night,
lighting the stable where he lay.
In his mother's arms he was laid to rest
as the breath of oxen warmed the air.
Then shepherds came from the hills nearby,
to kneel at his feet and adore
the promised one who had come at last,
and was laid on a stable floor.
Then the whole world hushed
for a moment in time
when the Bethlehem baby was born,
and his mother shed a quiet tear
as three great kings looked on.

AN UNEXPECTED DELIVERY

D r O'Reilly's small waiting room was almost full when the door swung open, and the Boyles swept in. I suppose I should say Mrs Boyle swept in, followed by her husband. But to tell the truth he was sucked relentlessly in, in her wake, like a fly caught in the whirling water when a bath plug is released.

She sailed across the crowded room towards the last remaining chair and settled herself. The chair shifted and groaned as her ample hips overflowed its frame. Mr Boyle, meanwhile, stood behind her, his back pressed against the surgery wall.

Mrs Boyle's button black eyes darted round the room, and I could see her assessing the reason for each person's visit. Some of the patients shrank from her gaze, while others buried their heads in the ancient magazines.

Some devilment possessed me and I met her stare head on. "Hello, Mrs Boyle" I said brightly, "And how are you today?" My words dropped like marbles in the quiet room, bouncing noisily into the expectant hush. Mrs Boyle swerved slowly and majestically to meet my eye. Meanwhile heads had lifted, and ears quivered like antennae. Everybody waited for her reply, yet it was plain as the nose on your face that Mrs Boyle was pregnant.

"I'm here for a check-up" she replied. "Not that it's anyone else's business." People exchanged meaningful glances as she lifted a magazine with a flourish. Meanwhile a slow tide of red was creeping up Mr Boyle's neck, as he cringed against the wall. Perhaps he was reading the thoughts of the company, wondering how he had managed, after all these years, to impregnate the formidable Mrs Boyle.

I smiled to myself, as I knew better, and I returned to setting up the patients' files, in readiness for their consultation. Eventually it was Mrs Boyle's turn to see the doctor. She sailed up to my desk and grabbed her file, directing a withering glance at me as she headed for the surgery door, followed by her meek husband.

Now it was open season in the waiting room. Comments flew from one to another, and a few choice remarks were made about Mrs Boyle's condition, but I pitied the child to come, and wondered how it would cope with such a formidable parent.

In this world there is nothing as certain as birth and death. Three months later the waiting was over. The mother went into labour early in the day, and Mrs Boyle's child arrived in the late evening of March 1st, the doctor having delivered a fine strapping boy.

As she was totally exhausted after the birth, Mrs Boyle did not see him immediately. Her husband was urgently called into the nursery, where he eagerly inspected the child. Ashen faced, he collapsed backwards into a chair, and then sought the doctor's face, searching wildly for some explanation. Helping Mr Boyle to his feet, the doctor led him gently into his office. Here he consulted his files, and then talked earnestly to the shaken father. A nurse pressed a hot cup of tea into the new father's trembling hands while phone calls were hurriedly made to the appropriate consultant in the hospital in Belfast who eventually was able to throw some light on the situation.

Some hours later Mr Boyle slowly entered the side ward where his wife lay. He found her somewhat recovered, freshened up and eager to hear details of their new son. "Well, Henry, what do you think of the little fellow? Who does he favour? I have repeatedly asked that nurse to bring him from the nursery, what on earth is keeping them?"

Henry held her plump hand and gently explained the situation to her. As he spoke, a look of horror transfixed her face. He pulled her into the circle of his arms and she cried as if her heart would break. Eventually she stopped, and they held one another in the silence of the room.

Heaving herself up in the bed Mrs Boyle spoke decisively. "I want to see him immediately!" she cried. "He is my baby, and I want to see him right now!" Mr Boyle rang the bell, and asked the nurse to bring in the child immediately. The nurse carried the child to mother and laid him carefully on the bed. Mrs Boyle gathered him into her ample arms, lifted back the blanket he was wrapped in, and examined him tenderly.

The child's large black eyes seemed to meet his mother's equally black eyes. Then he stretched, and somehow grasped her outstretched finger with his fat little hand. "What a grip he has," she said fondly as she met Mr Boyle's questioning gaze. A new softness lit her face as she stroked the baby's black fuzz of hair. "Henry, did you notice he has my eyes?" she smiled. Her husband returned her smile fondly. In the late evening sunlight the baby's skin glowed with health, and it was as polished and black as ebony. The baby yawned, and closed his remarkable eyes, curving naturally towards his mother. She responded, holding him close between her breasts. She rocked gently, a look of pure fulfilment on her face, and then she spoke. "Henry, I don't give a fig what mix up they've made with the donor sperm, and I couldn't care less what people will think or say! Who could resist this wonderful gift son of ours?"

Five days later they brought their new son home. She was true to her word and was a better-liked woman for it, parading up and down the town, like a proud battleship in full sail, with baby Emmanuel gurgling in his big Silver Cross pram.

BOUVIER DES FLANDRES

"War dog! War dog!" he called to you,
that ancient soldier in the park.
In his eyes he saw again your ancestors
pulling the bloody and the maimed
from muddy battlefields of Flandres.
Wrinkled hands held your great head
as he murmured his secret memories,
feeling their strong hearts beat again.
But you are carefree this spring day,
drunk on the scents and sounds of May
running through mysterious woods,
built like the tanks your breed
followed in the war to end all wars.
Above the grey ribbon of the Lagan
you gallop carefree among sappy bluebells,
huge paws thudding through tall grasses,
elephant ears flying as you charge,
in love with freedom, life, and me.

In the 1914 – 1918 war, Bouvier Des Flandres dogs
were used to pull injured troops away from the trenches on low carts,
beneath the poison gas and firing line of battle.

CAVEHILL 1947

Unforgiving terrain.
Ogre of my childhood.
Its sheer bulk
shadowing my shoulder,
sulking and fuming
brooding and bruising
the leaden sky,
resenting the scraggy heathers
clinging to its side.
I walk away
eyes wide.

BIG MAL

Big Mal, with his Lagan-wide smile
that charmed a rainbow range of friends
as diverse as his unique personality.
Shooting straight from the hip
with his lip
he popped the pompous with his dart of humour,
reducing us all to the ranks,
He ruled the kids with a rod of love,
and the odd gulder from his mighty lungs,
but Kitty knew his marshmallow centre
and soft beguiling words that melted the heart.
Now all are left,
bereft.

Written for Malachy Kielty,
with fond memories of a
wonderful and unique husband to Kitty,
father and a friend to all.

DEATH OF THE WOLFHOUND

Great hairy beast, wild and tempestuous,
unpredictable in your loving and giving,
you ruled my heart, my life, my soul.
Twisting and cajoling me to your way
with those wilful dark eyes,
running in mad unquestioning joy
long legs whirling, in your carefree dance
among the daffodils.
Great heaving chest, proud silhouette
against the grey Belfast sky,
your long jaw raised like a Lurgan spade,
scenting the air for a challenge!
Proud warrior, now fallen,
caught in a web of doom I cannot break,
dread foaming like a tide of alien blood
round and round my body,
searching for the neat solution,
not to be.
Dear dark face studded with eyes of question
and of pain, you look at me.
He comes with his needle to give the answer.
I hold your great hairy head in my hands,
easing your exit with soft words and kisses.
Peace comes in tandem flow with sedative,
spilling its answer through her veins.
Our heads lock, I am aware of her soft dead warmth,
the scent of her body mingling with mine.

It is over.

WRITERS' GROUP

Wendy came.

In time, she lifted the veil to her world.
Earth mother, feeling nature's vibrations,
tuned into the changing seasons,
she was the carefree beachcomber
wading the waters of Donegal, in Shaman fashion.
With her sisters she called out joyfully
into the void beyond Malin, where our world ends.
Running and laughing they spiralled out,
leaving a life print on the cool damp sand.
Now drifting from us,
her spirit wanders there,
lured by the azure Atlantic light
and the search to find her soul.

Wendy left.

CONAL

In those eyes of mysterious depths
I tremble when I hold his hand
tiny, clinging.
I see the magnitude of his trust,
the love in his heart.
And when my kisses mingle with the
sweet breath of innocence,
tears blind.

DEATH OF A FRIEND

There are no words between heaven and earth
to say how I feel about you, treasured friend.
Together we laughed, cried, grew close together,
sisters in the soul, matching warp and weft,

I am bereft.

SELECTION OF HAIKU

Yellow corn my couch
hot sun's handprint warm on back,
I am one with earth.

Paper shadow now,
you have gone, I must remain
silently screaming.

Carps bright head breaks through,
pink mouth wide, he gulps the food,
curve of orange, gone.

Dew trembling on leaf
mirrors this tear now falling
remembering you.

Relentless nature
pushing through the frozen earth
shocks us with colour.

The fly sips water,
resting on a green pond leaf
Frog grabs, life goes on.

White Jasmine's sweet scent
filling the moonlit terrace
captures and cajoles.

Crescent of black cat
curving on warm sunlit ledge
yawns, then sleeps once more

Spider in my bath
fails to climb his mountain slope
rescued now with love.

Yellow mixed with red
will make a startling orange
shocking pure white page.

Ground swell of bluebells
carpeting this woodland floor
spills colour everywhere.

Rich black earth turning,
yielding up this seasons crop.
The cycle goes on.

Lion crouches, alert,
dust rising from tufted mane,
flanks trembling, he springs.

EVERY DOG SHALL HAVE ITS DAY

James stood on the doorstep of the neat villa. Pressing the bell he shifted uncomfortably, dreading the coming encounter. Mrs Bingham had pulled back the lace curtain and was inspecting him before opening the door. He could tell she was surprised to see him, and he wondered if she even recognised him.

She eventually opened the door. "Good afternoon, Mrs Bingham", James began. "Come inside at once and state your business in private!" she interrupted, waving him towards the drawing room on the right. Inside, she settled herself on the sofa, but made no attempt to invite James to sit down. "Now, why are you here in the middle of the day?" she demanded, "Has my husband sent you to fetch some papers?" She looked up at him for the answer. James quailed at the task before him.

"Mrs Bingham, I am dreadfully sorry to bring bad news to your door. Sadly, Mr Bingham has had a fatal heart attack at the bank, in his own office. We tried our best as well as the ambulance men, but nothing could be done for him."

James stood looking down at her, feeling completely inadequate, and unsure what to do next. It was impossible to gauge her reaction – her face impassive, her body still. Then she lifted a soft rug and wrapped it around her body, as if to protect her against the shocking news he had brought.

James listened to the big Grandfather clock ticking loudly in the corner of the overheated room. A band of sweat forming inside his starched white collar as he stood stiffly waiting on her reaction. Now that he had imparted the bad news he wanted to escape but he knew he had to observe the formalities and be sympathetic. He had his position in the bank to safeguard, junior though it was.

Maybe Mrs Bingham would show her appreciation of his concern by putting in a good report of him at a later date. After all, he had served her husband well these last seven years – "Yes sir, no sir, three bags full, sir." Many a time he had felt like telling crusty old Bingham just where to go, but caution won the day. There was no chance of promotion if you let them see the whites of your eyes, no sir, keep your head down over the ledgers and be all things to your man – that was the way to promotion, he hoped!

With a start he realised Mrs Bingham was speaking to him. "Can you tell me what arrangements have been made?" she said. James looked at her florid face. At least she was in the land of the living! Kindly he patted her plump hand and spoke "Don't worry about anything, the bank has taken all steps necessary. A doctor was in attendance and Mr Bingham has been taken to the funeral home. We have also informed the family solicitor, who will be calling in tomorrow morning. Now is there any close relative I could contact for you?

Mrs Bingham blew her nose and unexpectedly grasped James's hand. "No, dear boy, you have been so kind and I'm sure you are anxious to get back to the bank." James accepted his cue gladly and made his escape from the dark stuffy room. The front door clicked behind him, leaving him wondering what would happen now.

Mrs Bingham sank down on the sofa and tried to control the emotions that swamped her totally. They seemed to take over her whole body, her shoulders shook and she doubled up. One hand flew to her mouth while the other clasped her ample stomach. Strange noises came from her mouth and she could no longer control her actions. Peals of laughter burst from her mouth as she heaved and shook on the sofa. She lay back and luxuriated in her sense of freedom.

Dipping her hand into the little crystal bowl of violet creams on the coffee table, she contemplated the future now the old skinflint was gone. She never suspected that he had a heart complaint. "Wonders will never cease!" she exclaimed to the silent room. "Now I shall live and do exactly as I please." She thought of the years spent in this dull provincial town and shuddered. Definitely there was a major change due in her life.

She flicked back the rug and headed for the bureau by the window. Pressing her first finger firmly beneath the ledge, she heard the little click that signalled the opening of the concealed drawer. She giggled as she swung it open. In all the years he had never suspected that she knew about his secret hidey-hole! Well, he was too late now to find out!

Her fingers groped around and slid out the walnut inlaid box. Opening the lid she was aghast to discover it empty. She frantically turned to the secret drawer and urgently searched every corner of it. With mounting panic she went through the entire contents of the bureau but there was nothing of any significance to be found. A rising panic gripped her heart and she felt she was no longer in control of the situation.

"Calm down, calm down, sit and think this out" she said to herself. There must, there had to be a logical explanation, the bankbooks must be somewhere safe. Reggie would have been too careful to allow anything to get misplaced.

Feeling a little better, she reached for the decanter of port on the bureau and poured a ' bumper' into a glass. A few sips and she began to go over everything again. Perhaps he had taken the books to the bank so that he could make the deposits more quickly, or, he felt they would be safer there instead of in the house. There was usually a logical answer to most problems. She stuffed the heap of receipts and paperwork back into the bureau – she would sort them tomorrow.

Enjoying the warm glow of the port, she was reassured. In fact, she thought, wouldn't another glass be so restorative? After all port was medicinal and was often recommended for shock. The sound of the radio drifted in from the kitchen as she made her plans. A weather report came on, more rain, then some waffle about a big donation to the local dogs home. Music from the 40's helped her to drift into a light sleep.

Next morning, as promised, the family solicitor arrived. He was wondering what state Mrs Bingham would be in today, but she greeted him warmly and invited him into the drawing room. She looked expectantly at him as he shuffled the papers. "Mrs Bingham," he began, "I have here your late husband's effects and papers i.e. his bank books, accounts and a personal letter addressed to…" "Oh, that's the mystery solved!" she interrupted. "I was so worried about the saving accounts and investments, yet I was sure Reggie would never have misplaced them – but who is the letter for?" The solicitor placed the letter on the table beside her, "Why, it's addressed to you, Mrs Bingham, to be handed to you on the death of your husband."

Mrs Bingham was wondering how she could get rid of the solicitor as she was dying to inspect the bankbooks and mystery letter. She wiped away a tear and said, "Would you mind completing our discussion tomorrow – I'm sure you understand, meanwhile I'll look over all this and we can see what needs urgent sorting out?" After accompanying the solicitor to the door she darted back into the drawing room. She had the bankbooks at last! Choosing one, she opened it at the last page, only to discover the words –Account closed – and a zero balance recorded. Frantically, she checked the others but the cashiers neat little figures told it all – there was no money, no money whatsoever. A low moan of fury and denial broke the silence and then she grabbed the letter. Maybe there would be an explanation, which would make sense. Tearing open the letter she began to read.

Dear Gertrude,

By the time you get this letter I will have "shuffled off this mortal coil" as they say. The doctor seems very surprised that I have lasted so long, with such a dickey heart! I have to tell you, sadly, that all the accounts are somewhat similar to Mother Hubbard's Cupboard – bare! Seemingly I am full of sayings today! Fortunately, the canine world has benefitted from my actions.

Let's face it Gertrude, you were beastly to me, and worst of all, denied me chick or child. How I would have treasured a little boy or girl and how one would have brightened our dull lives. But you said "NO" just as you said "NO" to that lovable stray pup all those years ago. Pleading with her eyes for any sort of a home and a few kind words. Yet, you chased her away. I would have cherished that little dog, but you said "NO" as always.

Then I realised that I could say "Yes, Yes, Yes" to donating my hard earned money to the care and protection of future strays, not to mention present residents in our local dog shelter. All will be provided for, making the memory of those pleading eyes a little easier to bear. My gift was made in cash, irrevocable and final. As is my last observation, Gertrude, that is "Every dog shall have its day."

FOOLS' DIAMONDS

Sparkling raindrops tremble on green leaves,
truly a "Hatton Garden" morning.
They catch in wobbly strings along the
clothesline,
then roll around in nasturtium leaves below,
the fools' diamonds I remember from
my childhood days.
Drop by drop they fill the mossy crock.
Soon birds swoop down to bathe.
A blackbird tangos back and forth.
The grey pigeon jumbos in,
red feet outstretched for splash down.
Next comes the magpie,
a regency buck in fine blue velvet
strutting on elegant legs to claim
his place.
Relentless rain beats down once more.

FOR ROSEMARY

This frost of pain has numbed me.
Black sorrow has overwhelmed me.
My dearest friend has gone.
Generous in her love and time, she was there
to help me over the hard stones of life,
plaiting the threads of true friendship
into an invincible rope of trust.
We shouldered the good times and the bad, together.
In these desperate days, sorrow coils in my heart.
I ask the question why she ripened like a flower,
then, in full bloom, was taken from us.
But only God can tell.

A NEW LIGHT OUT OF AN OLD MOON

Seamus sat rocking while he smoked the last pipe of the day. He was waiting to hear the key turn in the door, and see his son safely in for the night. He was an economical shape of a man, his body honed to a hard leanness by the years of work on the mountain. Often he wondered where those years had fled to. It seemed to him that it was only yesterday that he had been the young fellow, larking about and starting to work the farm with his own Da. In those days, Saturday night had been the highlight of the week, eagerly looked forward to by him and all the local lads.

Smiling and puffing, he remembered how it had been then, the men eagerly lining one side of the dance hall, and the girls on the other. Then a fellow knew where he was, with plenty of other hopefuls to take the bad look off him, as they sized up the talent. The girls pretending not to notice the men, chatting to one another, adjusting their ponytails, and shaking out their big frilly skirts, while they waited for the rush across the floor.

In those days his Ma always pressed his good blue Sunday suit on the Saturday afternoon. When he had finished the evening milking he put a sheet of newspaper on a kitchen chair and polished hell out of his black shoes. His Da said clean shoes showed a bit of breeding, and were the mark of a gentleman. He also maintained that a good gob of spit mixed with the polish gave a superior shine, so Seamus gave them the full treatment. Then he went into the scullery for a good sluice at the jaw box before he dressed for the dance. In his mind's eye he could see himself as he was then, cheeks pink from the rough towel, and his tow coloured hair standing up like a cock's comb, before he disciplined it with a wee dab of his Da's pomade. Those were the days!

He nursed the warm pipe. The young ones nowadays hadn't a clue about enjoying themselves, dressed like corner boys and sitting about in bars, ready to fall into bad company. He felt the familiar jag of worry about Tom. He hoped the cub, young as he was, would meet a nice wee girl soon. Seamus knew the lad wasn't the sharpest knife in the drawer, but he would always have the farm after his day, and he would be capable of managing that. It was a pity he was such a hot head, and so easily led. That was a recipe for trouble, and with the kind of boyos hanging about the town he could fall in with the wrong sort all too easily.

The mantel clock struck twelve, and he heard the bed creak above him as Annie turned in her sleep. Earlier he could see all the signs of worry on her, the ritual tidying and cleaning that gave her secret thoughts away. He hated to see her upset and had coaxed her to go on up. Annie was as dear to him now as she had been all those years ago. It was always Annie he had charged across the dance floor to claim as his partner. He had had his eye on her since their school days and was determined that no other fellow would get a look in.

Now he remembered how beautiful she had looked that first night he had kissed her. He could picture her still, standing by her father's gate, the night wind moulding the dress to her young body. The elderflower bushes had been in full bloom and their heady scent was overpowering. On an impulse he had picked a lacy spray of it and tucked it into the dark red strands of her hair. Then he had kissed her, drowning in the softness of her mouth and the perfume of the bruised flowers in her hair.
After that there was no one else but Annie, and they were married on Annie's twenty-first birthday.

It was nine years later that Tom had been born. Seamus had resigned himself to being childless, but Annie didn't give in so easily. She stormed heaven, demanding an answer to her prayers. Candles were lit and Novenas said, and water was taken from holy wells all over the country. On Easter Sunday 1962 the longed for baby was born, and they called him Thomas. Annie had picked that name in thanksgiving, for she said she was like Thomas, the disciple, doubting and questioning that she would ever have a child.

She threw herself into the role of mother wholeheartedly and Seamus felt the draught. He didn't want her to think he was jealous of the child but he sorely missed the intimacy of their former years. As the boy grew older and more independent Annie still fussed about him, reluctant to let him spread his wings. Like many another Irish mother she found it hard to snip the apron strings. Now he had taken to staying out late, and Annie couldn't handle the worry of it all. The situation had upset the balance of their lives and undercurrents washed away the peace in the house.

Seamus dozed in the chair, lulled by the heat of the fire. The chime of the clock brought him sharply awake. "God Almighty" he thought. "It's two in the morning and where the hell is that pup? I'll skin him alive for putting this heartache on us!" He poked the fire to raise some heat and waited on. When the first pink streaks of dawn were fingering the sky he heard the scrape of the lad's boots on the gravel outside. "Where the hell have you been to this time of night?" he hissed at Tom as he closed the door. Tom reacted to his father's anger with a surly "out!"

Seamus leapt from the chair, his face flushed with rage. "Out! I know only too well you were out, but out where and who with? Show a bit of respect, you ignorant pup, and answer the question. Where were you to this time of night?" He waited. "I was with a few friends and I wasn't watching the bloody clock every minute like a wee fella going home for his tea! You'd think I was a child the way you and my Ma carry on." Tom shouted. "Quit that roaring" Seamus spat out the words vehemently.

"Your mother's heart is broken enough as it is, with your carrying on. Hanging about some back lane with a lassie, up to no good, that's where you've been, if the truth were told!" The young fellow looked at the father's furious face and clenched fists and decided to back peddle, "Da, you worry far too much about me! I can take care of myself. Sure here I am as safe as houses and dying to get to my bed! Tomorrow we'll need to move the sheep down to the bay field. Let's get our heads down while we can." He paused at the door and when Seamus made no move, he closed it gently behind him.

Seamus slumped down into the chair, conscious of the blood pumping furiously round his body. He listened to the feet padding about upstairs, followed by the click of the light switch. "Jesus," he thought. "I'd need to watch myself, or I'll be having a heart attack! Thank God Annie didn't hear the row." Suddenly he felt old and vulnerable, and doubted if he could handle the situation. After a few minutes of brooding, he went upstairs and slipped into the bed beside Annie. Warmed by her body he fell into a deep sleep.

Over the next few months the father and son shared an uneasy truce. Seamus was so anxious to spare Annie he said nothing about the lad's late hours, but Annie wasn't fooled. She began to keep the nightly vigil with him as he waited up for the boy, questioning and torturing herself until Seamus could stick it no longer. The next night the lad came in late he exploded with anger. Bitter words and accusations were exchanged, and Tom slammed out the door. Annie sat on the couch, rocking and weeping. Seamus tried to ease her heartache by telling her the lad would be back on the morning "as large as life and twice as handsome." Annie smiled through her tears as he took her up to bed. There he held her in his arms until she fell into an exhausted sleep.

Tom did not come home for five days. His father made enquiries but failed to find out where he had been during that time. In desperation, Annie pleaded with him to let the boy keep whatever hours he liked, in the hope that he would stay at home. To keep the peace Seamus agreed, and got on with the work of the farm. Tom pulled his weight, doing a fair share of the chores. He said little and kept himself to himself, and Seamus wondered at the change in him.

Usually at night he left the house without speaking to them but that Saturday evening he surprised them by coming into the kitchen "Well Ma, I'm away out" he said, bending to kiss her cheek. He passed behind Seamus's chair, trailing his fingers across his father's shoulders. "Good night Da." he said, and left the room. It was the first sign of affection they had seen in him for six months. Seamus was puzzled but flushed with pleasure at the gesture. "Well, that's a new light out of an old moon!" he laughed, covering his confusion. Annie was positively glowing. "Maybe he has a wee girl in the town! Mark my words, he'll be bringing changes round here before we know it! Wouldn't a wedding be grand?" They passed a pleasant evening together, Seamus indulgently listening to Annie's happy chatter about love affairs and weddings and grandchildren. Happy and contented they went up to bed.

Seamus sat bold upright when he heard the hammering at the door. Annie stirred in the bed and moaned in her sleep. "Damn and blast," Seamus muttered, "That cub has forgotten his key again!" He slipped quietly out of bed and went down to let his son in. The big R.U.C. man filled the doorway, while another stood behind him. Seamus recognised the big man, they had sat together in the classroom of the National School all those years ago, when all the children went to the one school in the village. Strangely though, their paths had not crossed until now. "Could you come with us?" the Sergeant said, "there has been an accident." Seamus could feel the fear crawling like an animal in the pit of his stomach, yet he could not move. The Sergeant waited, thinking of his own sons. The young Constable accompanying him moved restlessly, wondering why he was pussyfooting round this man, whose eegit of a son was lying dead outside the Barracks with his misguided pals. Hadn't he got what he deserved? If he hadn't got involved with that lot he would be alive now. He stepped forward impatiently. Seamus turned and gently closed the door. He walked with the two men to the car wondering what he would say to Annie.

KATIE A

Hey Katie A,
You were really classy
sharp as a tack,
dressin smart and sassy!
Wowing the guys, makin ladies sigh
as you whirled to show a flash of thigh,
marking you out as someone really special
putting the rest of us dolls on our mettle.
Shoes 'n bags 'n hats 'n dresses
and a coiffeur straight from top
hairdressers.
You sashayed down to Belfast city where
passers-by called "aint she so pretty!"
Wolf whistles showed the guys' appreciation
and you were the centre of every
celebration!
The years may have passed
but Katie still could cut it –
full of craic, memories and dry wit!
With the crossing of gazelle legs
you revived all that glamour,
with your tales of past times
you could silence all the clamour,
and I know for certain now
in heaven up above
you are holding court
surrounded still by love,
with God on your right
and family on your left,
you don't give a damn
about leaving us bereft!!

In memory of Kate Alexander,
her family and all her friends in
Ballynafeigh Writers Group
June 2007

97

END OF THE DAY

I'm tucked up in bed, and feeling grand,
Strong tea and soda bread in my hand.

Door closed tight, bloody visitors gone,
The scullery locked, the curtains are drawn.

The fire's banked up, wet slack packed in tight
With a bit of luck it should last through the night.

To fend off the draught, I've wrapped up me head
In an old woolly jumper, now faded red.

There's always great warmth in a hand knit
So I wrap it round tightly, for a snug fit.

My Rosary's recited, the Novena is said –
Just in case I'm caught short, the po's under the bed!

With a few drops of Dettol just under the rim
To banjax the germs that are lurking within.

Me teeth's in the mug by the side of the bed,
The corsets rolled up and tucked under me head.

What have I forgotten? I throw back the cover
Swallow a wee tot and then

Dive back under!

QUEEN BEE

Quirky Kate,
queen bee of Graffiti society
I see you still.
Ruby wine glinting,
smoke spiralling,
long legs elegantly curled
as you read your stories
to the great and the good.
Surrounded by five daughters
and adoring friends
we celebrate your eight decades,
unaware of the shadow slowly falling.
In these last weeks we
had treasured our times together,
me curling your hair,
Linda smiling and chatting,
Maria making the tea,
and you, to that last moment,
still the queen bee.

Written for my dear
friend Kate Alexanderand her family.

MAGGIE'S ADVICE

They say that it's time to go into a Home
That now it's not safe to be here on me own!

I look at their faces, so full of concern
And think to myself they've a lot still to learn!

The kitchen may look like a sheugh in a storm
But the old range is turf packed, to keep meself warm.

It glows roaring red, and throws out a great heat,
With the wellies pulled off, I toast the auld feet.

Then I steep them in water, topped up with some Daz –
I wouldn't swap turf for yon new-fangled gas!

Me socks are washed out, they were clean full of muck,
the clabber seeped in when I fell in the sheugh.

I was chasing auld Daisy down by the barn
When I slipped on a cowpat, but came to no harm.

Sure there's nothing like putting your trust in your God
Since he made all of us, just like the turf sod.

These auld Welfare biddies just haven't a clue
They think I'm at death's door, with only a flu!

A poultice of mustard clapped onto the chest
And a hot tot of whisky, I find is the best!

To hell and to Connaught with their antibiotic –
Me Grannie's old cures are the very best tonic!

Now I've brushed the biscuit crumbs out of the bed
An old flannel nightie is wrapped round me head

To kill more of the germs I'll just smoke a last pipe,
Then with all the prayers said, I'll just blow out the
light.

PYLON PEOPLE

Rigid in your ordered existence
I hear you calling out in supplication,
thin arms out stretched, gaunt and black
against this pink dawn
screaming words down taut wires
I wonder who is even listening…

"ROUGE BONNET" A LA BARBARA CARTLAND

Rouge Bonnet lay on her counterpane and thought about life. Today was her sixteenth birthday, and her mind and heart were full of turmoil. Rolling over, she rested her head on her lavender pillow. Luxuriously she stretched, revealing the delicate budding curves of her firm young body. Since her family had come as émigrés to escape the terrors of the Revolution, she had led a sheltered and lonely life. The fact that she was an only child compounded the problem, Mamma and Papa still treated her as "La petite", the "Little one", and she wondered if they would ever accept her growing into a woman.

She could not confide in Mamma! She dared not reveal the strange longings, the swirl of emotions and the changing moods that swamped her daily. If Mamma knew how she indulged in these delicious imaginings, sighing and dreaming the hours away, she would be scandalised! Rouge jumped up, she would confide in her darling Grandmamma! She would trust her, bare her soul and take her advice!

Rouge sat before her mirror to brush her hair. A faint reflection moved in the glass. Whirling, she turned to look out the window. It was indeed William, the woodcutter. How handsome and manly he looked! How proud and strong! As he swung his axe, the muscles swelled beneath his tanned arms. A little sigh came from her lips.

"Rouge!" her mother called. "Hurry down and take these little treats to your Grandma. Remember not to speak to anyone in the forest." Rouge put on her scarlet woollen cloak, picked up the basket and set off. As she walked she peeked shyly from under the red hood. Sure enough William was following her with his eyes. Rouge felt a flutter in her heart, but just waved shyly and walked on.

Another less welcome pair of eyes was also watching, full of base desire and brutish intent. This was Lupus, an evil wolfish character who lived a solitary life in the forest. Day after day he spied on Rouge, intent on possessing the beautiful young girl.

Seizing his opportunity he raced ahead to Grandma's cottage. Slipping silently inside, he quickly overpowered his unsuspecting victim and pushed her into a cupboard beneath the stairs.

He ran to the bedroom, pulled the Grandmother's peignoir on and covered his head with her frilly mobcap. Then he slid into the bed, pulling the eiderdown up to cover his hairy chin. Rouge came upstairs, anxious to confide in her dear Grandmamma and to seek advice in these matters of the heart.

However, she was shocked to see a great deterioration in her condition, and with deep concern said "Grandmamma, what big eyes you've got today!" Lupus lay in the bed, eyes as big as saucers with desire.

"All the better to see you with ma Cherie!" he replied. "Dear heart," said Rouge, "What big ears you've got." "All the better to hear your loving voice," said Lupus. By now he was wild with desire and his longing for Rouge. He began to pant, revealing his great yellow teeth as his hot breath scorched the air, "all the better to taste your cherry lips, to nibble your little pink ears, to…" Rouge's scream rent the air, rising and falling with the panic within her breast. A wave of revulsion swept over her as he caught her by the wrist. Twisting and turning she struggled to escape the awful fate that awaited her.

She could feel his hot, sour breath on her cheek; see the wild longing in his cold green eyes as he held her in his grasp. With a crash, the bedroom door flew open – it was William! A sob escaped her lips "Help me, help me!" she cried. William sprang to the bed and raising his axe in a mighty arc he ended her nightmare.

Shielding her from the awful sight he swept her up into his strong arms. She could feel his heart beating against hers as he held her in his embrace. Gently, he kissed her cheek. "Dear little Rouge," he said. "I am so glad I got here in time to save you, and return you to your parents unharmed." My dearest friend Rupert is keeping watch outside. We knew Lupus had evil intentions towards you. We always looked out for you as we took our walks together in the forest.

Rouge loosened her grip on handsome William's arm as she became aware of the situation.

There would be no passionate love story in her young life yet…

SANCTUARY

In this calm white room I paint,
watching the reflected world,
green canopied trees, tissue clouds,
a pattern of birds marking the blush canvas
of the early morning sky.
The mirror captures it all,
as the murmuring clock marks time
till night comes in black velvet,
and white lilac perfumes the darkened room.

SEAMUS AND JOANNE'S WEDDING DAY

Treasure this love, make it your own
mould it as the potter shapes clay,
as a sculptor carves stone.

Nourish, protect and keeping it close,
watch as it flourishes, blossoms, grows
gifting this love to those you love most.
Share your healing with one another
pooling knowledge and compassion,
caring as a mother, sister, brother.

May a garland of children encircle your life
bringing joy and fulfilment,
far from illness or strife.

In their turn may your children bring,
cradled in strong arms, new life,
joyous as spring.

Then at life's end may you grow old together,
passing from this world, entwined together.

Treasure this love, make it your own
mould it as the potter shapes clay
as a sculptor carves stone.

THE DONKEY

I heard a footfall at the door of the stable,
Then their shadows danced on the wall.
The light of the lantern playing its tricks
made these two seem ten feet tall.

But when she sank down beside me
her blue gown billowing around
I saw she was only a slip of a girl,
curled up in the straw on the ground.

A soft moan I heard in the stillness.
Her head sought the warmth of my side
and a baby was born in the darkness
as the man held the hand of his bride.

My breath hovered over the baby,
as mist in the cold night air.
Gently enfolding the Saviour
as the man and his wife said a prayer.

SAINT PATRICK'S EVE.   MARCH 16th 2003

Like a Celtic warrior he was armed for his journey,
misty glass angel in his pocket,
and the water of life in another.
By his left hand we laid a shillelagh,
symbolic staff to steady him on the path
of those who had gone before.
In his right hand the images of Lara and Finn,
his faithful Great Danes,
to guard and guide him to that other world.
Then the soft words of cherished children
were pillowed beneath his feet.
A spray of shamrock we laid on his breast,
symbol of faith and the land he so loved.
Last of all, blessed water,
and this poem to record his passing.

In memory of
My brother- in- law
Michael Blaney.

SONG OF THE UNBORN

I know not the time of my coming
but welcome me into your harsh daylight
or the dim darkness of your night.
Ease my coming with soft words and touches.
Bathe me in warm waters, wrap me in white velvet
Lap me in love.
Hold me, caress me, examine my completeness.
Breathe my breath; share my new life with me.
Count my perfections, the nails on my hand,
every hair on my head.
Endlessly gaze on me, drinking me in.
Laugh with me, cling to me.
Now is the time, be glad I have come.

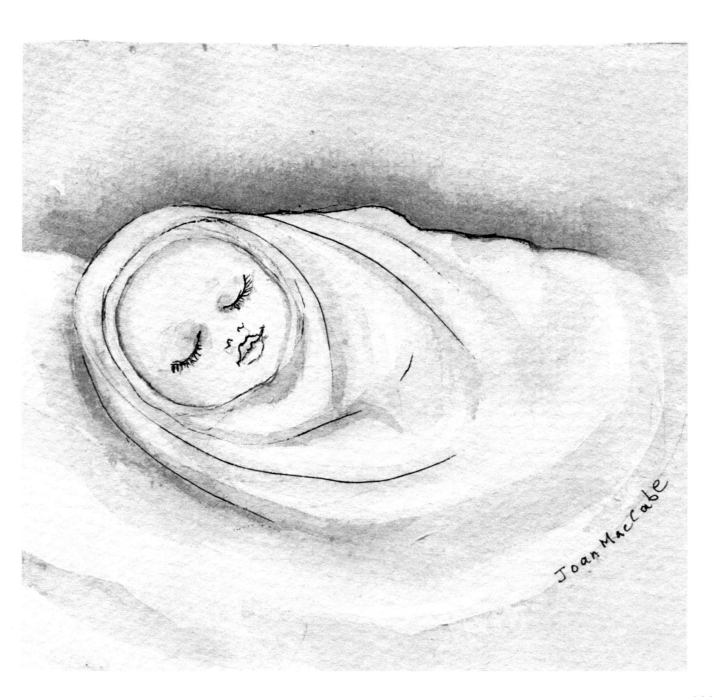

Joan MacCabe

THE HERON

Beneath the Ormeau Bridge the heron stands
in inky Lagan water, still as glass.
Elegant on ballet dancers legs,
his watchful eye on me as here I pass.

I stop, and echoing his stance, keep still
I hold my breath, entranced, I drink him in.
standing in mysterious morning mist
this perfect creature, with reflected twin.

THE MARINER

Perhaps at the horizon, he may once again look back
at us distant dots on the sand,
then rush to the welcoming arms
of those who now reach for his hand.
Beaching then on Heavens' shore,
with a fair wind at his back,
he sails the seven seas no more,
now his anchor rope is slack.
The endless journeys are now done,
hard work and suffering over.
This day his paradise is won,
home at last, salt water rover.

In memory of Michael Blaney,
who spent his life sailing
the seas all over the world.

BAGGING IT

Fat bags, slim bags.
Filled up to the brim bags!
Purple bags, yellow bags
make up spilling out bags.
Posh bags, moneybags.
Strapped around the tummy bags.
Small-embroidered antique bags.
Ancient battered shopping bags.
Silver bags, evening bags,
golden thread and glitter bags.
Smell of leather, sporty bags,
fishing bags, sandwich bags,
egg and onion smelling bags
Worst of all? My under eye bags!

THE BALLAD OF NO-KNICKS NELL

Nell surveyed the distant quay,
and informed the Captain
"It's no knicks for me!"
"What's your problem?" he said with a frown,
"Just that your transport has let me down!
They've lost my luggage and all the rest
so from now on I think it best
to revert to nature –
let sea breezes keep me fresh!
Sure all yon bonny Scottish lads
survive the cold with just their plaids,
and we are heading for the sun
and breezy bums just might be fun!

Perhaps I'll even start a trend
and maybe meet a cheeky friend
who'll bounce about the decks with me
as we progress across the sea!"
"No knicks Nell" was the toast of the ship,
with no elastic strain at her hip,
as she sashayed both up and down
while disembarking at each town,
and though the rest were dressed to the hilt
Nell stayed loyal to a trendy wee kilt.
She ended up the belle of the ball
and never missed her knickers at all.

Marks and Spencer felt the draught
when she was finally home at last
for that taste of freedom on the cruise
was the catalyst that set her loose

from the confines of 'Directoire' knickers,
and now she's joined the can-can kickers!
With a flirt of her skirt
and a pout on her lip
She brings a new meaning to the word – "hip!"

Written for a friend
whose luggage went missing
at the beginning of her holiday cruise.

THE PASSING YEAR

Mischievous January, huffing and puffing,
blows up the skirts of February,
revealing a lacy edging of snowdrops.
March, light headed
skips through the windy park,
rippling the yellow daffodils as she runs.
April follows, eyes spilling crystal raindrops,
that soften the dark brown earth
and stud it with the early primroses.
Young May then dances in,
scattering pink cherry blossom,
a scented path beneath our feet.
Hot-blooded June, drowsy with the warmth of summer nights,
sleeps among her perfumed roses,
beneath an ink blue sky.
Indolent July curls up beneath the ripening corn,
a crown of butterflies
fluttering around her brow.
Waist deep in meadow grasses
August sways.
framed by wild flowers of white and blue
September tiptoes by the laden bushes,
kissing the sweet seductive fruit
with juice stained lips.
October comes, the artist,
painting the woods with orange, red and brown,
a colour palette for the young at heart.
Mysterious November glides along,
wrapped in a pale grey mist.
The Gretta Garbo month.
Then Diamond Lil, December,
with stars caught in her silver hair,
steps out to take the final bow.

THE SNAIL

Translucent traveller, high on the warm brick wall,
you have conquered your Everest.
Behind the green tracery of leaves you rest,
sheltered in the lace of evening sun and shadow.
I spy on you in your secret place,
marvelling at your epic journey.
Unaware of my presence, you stretch in a long graceful curve,
creating a pearl grey cameo in silhouette.
I can see the dimples on your plump body,
your delicate horns caressing the air,
and I am seduced by your fragile beauty.

"PUPPETEER"

Like the grim reaper following on,
despair stalks them, hunting them down.
Spread-eagled on the wasteland of their plight
he picks them, as his playthings of the night.
Helpless puppets dancing to his tune
they try to fight against his will but soon
they scream in silent voice that no one hears,
just echoes ringing, mirroring their fears.
Mocking their misery he now plays the clown,
dangling a solution – only to cast it down.
Out of their reach it disappears from sight
as on he postures through their dreary night.
They are dependant on his every whim,
caught in his claw, they submit to suffering.
They know of no solution, no escape
in foetal curves of fear, all now await their fate.

Dedicated to all
who battle depression.

TURNING POINT

Canon MacNeill visited the sick of the parish on the first Monday of every month. One of his regulars was Bridie's father, whose legs had been crushed in an accident on his farm. Bridie heard the heavy tread of the priest in the porch and the rasp of his boots on the iron foot scraper. Any visitor was welcome at the lonely farmhouse, so she ran down the hall to greet him. "Good day, Canon, you're very welcome! Come on in out of the cold. That wind would clean corn, as Mammy used to say!" Bridie's face was flushed and she giggled as she took the Canon's black hat and placed it reverently on the hallstand.

Canon MacNeill stood looking at her. She was a buxom lass with a fine head of dark red curls. Described unkindly by some in the village as, "not the sharpest knife in the drawer". Bridie had stumbled through school, and unable to take on a job, was now trying to run the farm for her father. "Well Bridie, do you still miss your Mammie as much as ever?" the Canon enquired. Bridie's face clouded over, and tears formed in her eyes. She gulped, but just couldn't express her feelings. She hung her head and twisted her apron into a ball. Canon MacNeill took the situation in hand. "Your Mammie is in a far better place. Do you believe me Bridie?" the Canon asked. "I do" Bridie replied, for that was the answer she thought would please him. "What about the Da? Is he up or down? In good form or bad?" said the Canon. "Well, he's just his usual self," said Bridie, wiping her nose on a crumpled hanky. "Sure go on down to the room and see for yourself". When they reached the door Bridie announced the priest. "Right Da, here's Cannon MacNeill to see you, coming all this way on such a bad day". "Cut the crap girl," said the voice from the bed. "You'll be giving him a big head about himself, he'll be looking for canonisation before we know it! Sit down, Paddy, and give us a bit of your craic, I'm going mad tied to these four walls and the farm falling apart!" Mr O'Brien beckoned to the chair beside the bed.

The Canon chuckled and eased himself into the chair. He looked at James O'Brien, to gauge the state of play, since his moods were as changeable as the weather, and he knew this man in the big old bed would instantly reject platitudes.

Meanwhile Bridie settled into the kitchen chair with her paperback romance. She hunkered forward to let the roasting heat from the range reach her soft white thighs. It hit her with a welcome blast and she revelled in its comfort. The house was always draughty and cold. She remembered her Mammie complaining, and her efforts to keep out the draughts by hanging heavy curtains over the door, but the icy wind still curled round their ankles and whistled through the rattling windows. Once or twice Bridie had tried to coax her father to get one of those new electric heaters, but he insisted that he had a bog full of the best of turf, and that it would do him his day. He had not foreseen the accident that would leave him unable to walk or ever work the turf again. Then Bridie's mother, Hannah, suddenly died the following January and the light went out in his world. Since then Bridie had carried on somehow, seeing to both the house and the farm. Before she had been free to roam the fields, but now everything depended on her. Most of all she hated the turf bog, with its bracken water seeping over the top of her boots and the stinging mountain rain driving into her face. Now, cosy and warm she opened her book, and keeping her finger on the line of words, she drank in the story of the lovers.

Down in the room the big priest spoke to the father, "Bridie's not coping too well, by the look of it", he ventured. 'What the hell can I do?" exploded James. "I'll hardly get a woman to take over a cripple like me, not to mention the responsibility of Bridie." "Calm down! Calm down!" said the priest, "What about taking on a young fellow with plenty of work in him?" James rose in the bed, his eyes on fire. "Where would I get the money for a man's wages? There's no way Bridie could hold down a job and bring money into the house!" The priest pressed his fingertips together and thought for a moment. "I still maintain a young lad would cost less. There's young Ned O'Connor, back from London and out of work. He'd be glad of a turn over the winter months!' James sat and considered the suggestion. Then he slapped the eiderdown, 'Right, Paddy!" he exclaimed, "you've convinced me! Will you speak to the lad and set it up? He could start immediately, and if he calls I'll settle the terms with him, and what I expect him to do." "I'll do that," said the Canon, pleased with his work that day. "Now man, get the Jameson out of the press, there, and pour us a noggin each," said James. "This left leg is pure purgatory to me today!" Canon MacNeill hid his smile and did as he was bid. Later he told Bridie of the new arrangement. She clapped her hands in delight. "Do you think this boy will cut the turf? I'm sick to death of that bog, I'd not miss it if I never saw it again!" "Settle yourself girl, and bring in the tea and cake," said her father, "This bucko will work for his money, and the turf cutting will at the top of his list".

Two days later Ned O'Connor was interviewed behind the closed door of the bedroom by Mr O'Brien. Bridie hovered about but heard nothing. Ned emerged to begin work on the farm. He was a quiet lad who said little and worked hard for his money, milking the cows, mucking out the byre and seeing to the fields. Bridie had more time now, and in her own way tried to improve the house, cleaning and polishing, remembering the way her Mammy had taught her. She even took down her mother's recipe book, and stumbling through it, tried to make some of their old favourites. Ned came in when he had finished work and shyly she offered him share.

She was delighted when he praised the apple tart, telling her he had never tasted the like of it in London. He talked about his life there, and the never-ending work of the building sites. As he talked Bridie watched him, admiring his thick flaxen hair, as yellow as the corn in the bottom field. Suddenly her father's bell rang and she ran to the room. "Yes Da, can I get you anything?" she said. "Yes, get that young cub on home! It's time he was on his way. Don't encourage him to dawdle about the kitchen once he has finished his work," her father grumbled. "Father, he'll hear you!" whispered Bridie. "What odds if he does?" said Mr O'Brien, as he switched on the wireless to hear the latest war news. Bridie returned to the kitchen, her cheeks blazing. Ned was smiling broadly. "I don't know what to say," ventured Bridie. He laughed. "Never mind your Da" he said "I'll just have to be very quiet when I come into the kitchen, and what he doesn't know won't harm him! Goodnight, Bridie" He patted her cheek and closed the door. Bridie listened as his footsteps faded down the lane. She felt a rush of queer sensations mixed with excitement wash over her. She liked it, but she couldn't understand it. That night she lay in bed, exhilarated, and looking forward to seeing Ned the next day.

Over the next few months Bridie was careful not to let her father know that Ned visited her after his work was done. She made sure her father had finished his evening meal and was tucked up with his glass of Jameson by six o'clock. She turned on the wireless at two minutes to six for the news, and if the volume was louder than unusual he didn't seem to notice, and he appreciated her thoughtfulness when she closed the door to keep out the draughts. He was well pleased with the arrangements, and the lad seemed to be working hard. On the Canon's next visit, he sounded out James. "Well, how is the lad working out?" he enquired. "Well enough", said James. "And Bridie seems to be catching on a bit better. Do you know she has even started to bake, now that she has a bit more time?" The door opened and Bridie came in with the tray. "Speak of the devil!" said her father "I was telling Canon MacNeill how well improved you are, Bridie." She flushed with pride, since her father was usually sparing in his praise of her. "I'm just trying to follow the recipes in Mammie's book," she said. "God bless your Mammie, she was the best baker in this town land", said the Canon.

When Canon MacNeill left, Bridie settled her father. As she walked to the kitchen she heard the click of the door as Ned came in. They sat quietly together at the front of the range, talking in low voices in case James would overhear them in the room beyond. Once he called up for a cup of water, but that was the only interruption. When Ned left that night Bridie walked down the lane with him. Suddenly Ned pulled her to him, kissing her awkwardly and burying his fingers in the thick redness of her hair. She clung instinctively to him, stirred into awareness by her first male kiss.

He responded to her eagerness, kissing her over and over again, and feeling the full softness of her body beneath his hands.

Bridie was driven by such a tumult of feelings and sensations yet the thought came to her that if her father knew what she was doing he would kill the two of them. Still the danger only seemed to heighten her intense pleasure and she clung to Ned, eager for the feel of his mouth on hers and wanting the sensation never to end.

That night was the turning point for Bridie. She could hardly wait for Ned to come in the door each evening and he was touched by her childlike adoration of him. Each evening they ventured a little further, exploring each other, and deepening the intensity of their need for one another. On the evening he first led her to her bedroom it seemed as natural as breathing to her. Sometimes she was overcome by the fear of the old man finding them out, but she pushed it out of her mind and clung to Ned. The long winter months passed in the frenzy of their passion and Bridie spent her days longing for the night to come. Ned caressed her, his hands exploring the planes of her body. Slowly he became aware of her fullness, a new ripening in her.

In the darkness he turned to her. "Bridie" he blurted out. "Do you think you are alright, I mean, could you be getting a baby?" Bridie laughed, kissed him and snuggled into his arms. "Don't be daft, Ned, sure you have to go into hospital to get a baby!" she said and then drifted into a carefree sleep.

Ned lay in shock, fully aware for the first time of the extent of Bridie's simplicity, and he knew he could never face her father, or the coming situation. On the following Friday night he took the eight o'clock boat to Liverpool, and travelled on to London the next day. Bridie quietly pined while her father raged at the loss of a good worker for no obvious reason. He sent for the Canon, who calmed him down and promised to see what he could do to replace Ned. Then he headed back to the kitchen. "Well Bridie" he said, "I think I've settled your Da, and I'm sure I can find another…" he stopped short as he caught Bridie's silhouette in the firelight, and he knew why Ned had gone. "Make us a cup of tea Bridie, and sit down with me," he said. When he had questioned her, and made sure of the facts, Canon MacNeill told her gently what was to come.

Bridie looked at him, first in disbelief, and then in terror. She whimpered and shrank back into the chair. The Canon patted her hand and spoke in a gentle comforting voice to her. "Bridie, we'll get you through this somehow, and I'll be the one to face your Da!" Bridie froze, her eyes standing out in her head. "No! No!" she whispered, "No-one must be told, no-one must tell". She rocked backwards and forwards in the chair, twisting her fingers this way and that. Suddenly she sprang to her feet.

"I need to go out and think about this, will you mind my Da?" "I will indeed," said the Canon soothingly. "I'll make him a wee cup of tea. You go out for a dander and calm yourself, Bridie, sure there's nothing that can't be solved with the help of God!" When the tea was made he took it and a slice of fruitcake down to face James with the coming problem.

Canon MacNeill was due at the chapel for confessions at seven o'clock. Fifteen minutes before the hour he was standing at the farmhouse door, impatiently scouring the lane for Bridie. "Where on earth has she got to?" he said, "And people waiting down below in the church!" He hurried down the lane to the Doherty's and asked the woman of the house to keep an eye on James until Bridie returned. Then he jumped on his bicycle and pedalled furiously towards the chapel. After confessions he decided to cycle back up to see James and maybe sit down with the pair of them and make some plans, since it would take a miracle to sort out this tangle. When he reached the farm he found Mrs Doherty still there, and James angry and silent.

The Canon wasted no time, responding to the knot of worry in his stomach. He hurried down the lane and collected the three Doherty sons and their father. On his way home from work one of the lads had seen Bridie running along the path by the bog. They spread out over the mountain, calling her name, while the lurcher dog ran excitedly between them. It was the priest who first saw her, lying in the resin brown bog water, her red hair floating all about her, and the December frost already caught in her lashes. It was black night when they carried her in the door of her father's house.

TWINS

I watch your sleeping faces, side by side,
caught in soft focus by the landing light.
Hands in surrender now, above your head,
baby breath marking time in this quiet room.

What dreams drift behind those sleeping eyes
caught and cocooned within your growing minds,
seeding in time, to burst like a ripening flower
from your pen, and the dancing words in your head.

Restless now in sleep, he seeks her matching hand.
In a careless tangle of limbs, they curl together.
Secure in their oneness, gene matched in time
they slumber on, a perfect society of two.

VICTIMS

I watch them flying through the air,
Participants in some black nursery rhyme.
Hey diddle diddle, lay them deep in the middle,
Body on body in the cold brown winter earth,
Deep in the pit I dug for them with trembling hands.
Smoke and smell rises now in choking unison
Writing its message of doom across the sky,
Filling my lungs with the stench of burning skin,
Those velvet flanks smoothed by these hands
This very morning.
I remember them crowding me, trusting me,
Hot sweet breath caught in the frosty morning air,
Feeling their soft pink mouths, moist against these hands.
Again the crane rises, and high above my head
A winter sun enriches a russet pelt.
It begins again.

Mad Cow Disease or BSE
as it was first called
appeared in 1986

ITALIAN BRIDE

In the trunk that came with her from Casalattico
Her precious garments still lie,
Returning to their former folds
Like long pressed flowers.
No longer needed, unheeded
They lie as she last layered them
Before those final days.
Beneath their high iron bed
That trunk still holds her presence,
And in the sadness of the night
His hand seeks comfort in
Caressing its smooth surface.
Once more, imagining that heady moment
When she arrived at Belfast docks.

BRENDAN

Up on Knockshee a man has a dream
of pure spirits sparkling like a stream
as once ancient distillers had captured in mid flow,
and mixed the ripened grains with it so long ago.
Standing by Kilfeaghan Dolmen he gave a mighty cry –
"Never will I let this great tradition die!
I'll build a place as timeless as this historic site
and mix and blend and bottle even through the night!
With dedication, love and inspiration my dreams
will now find fame throughout the nation".
In time the purest spirits came to pass
with peaty flavours, sparkling clear within the glass.
Two trusty stills he named Christoir and Broc
working in tandem, faithful as a rock
that stands in memory of people and times past
and hope Killowen will forever last.

Written for Brendan Carty
Founder of Killowen Distillery

JOURNEY'S END

He was a faint outline, barely there. Just a rickle of bones patterning the white sheet that covered him. I thought of the rubbings from warriors' tombs, the rich and detailed carving telling of their life cycle. Above the sheet his fluff of white beard was combed to lie in perfect order.

Sometimes the old one paused in her hovering to gently stroke it down against the white linen. I peered through childish fingers at the black rosary beads fencing his work-worn fingers, a legacy of a lifetime's toil in Leitrim soil.

The room was so silent, only his breath coming in soft uneven whistles. The adults encircled the iron bed and prayers were said. My mother held her father's wrist as the whistles grew slower, then took me to the door and eased me out. "Go and check on the hens in the wee shed" she whispered, and closed the door to the whitewashed bedroom.